Diary Methods for Personality and Social Psychology

The SAGE Library of Methods in Social and Personality Psychology is a new series of books to provide students and researchers in these fields with an understanding of the methods and techniques essential to conducting cutting-edge research.

Each volume explains a specific topic and has been written by an active scholar (or scholars) with expertise in that particular methodological domain. Assuming no prior knowledge of the topic, the volumes are clear and accessible for all readers. In each volume, a topic is introduced, applications are discussed, and readers are led step by step through worked examples. In addition, advice about how to interpret and prepare results for publication is presented.

The Library should be particularly valuable for advanced students and academics who want to know more about how to use research methods and who want experience-based advice from leading scholars in social and personality psychology.

Published titles:
James J. Blascovich, Eric Vanman, Wendy Berry Mendes & Sally Dickerson, *Social Psychophysiology for Social and Personality Psychology*

R. Michael Furr, *Scale Construction and Psychometrics for Social and Personality Psychology*

Rick H. Hoyle, *Structural Equation Modeling for Social and Personality Psychology*

John B. Nezlek, *Multilevel Modeling for Social and Personality Psychology*

Laurie A. Rudman, *Implicit Measures for Social and Personality Psychology*

The SAGE Library of Methods in Social and Personality Psychology

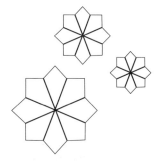

Diary Methods for Personality and Social Psychology

John B. Nezlek

Los Angeles | London | New Delhi
Singapore | Washington DC

Los Angeles | London | New Delhi
Singapore | Washington DC

SAGE Publications Ltd
1 Oliver's Yard
55 City Road
London EC1Y 1SP

SAGE Publications Inc.
2455 Teller Road
Thousand Oaks, California 91320

SAGE Publications India Pvt Ltd
B 1/I 1 Mohan Cooperative Industrial Area
Mathura Road
New Delhi 110 044

SAGE Publications Asia-Pacific Pte Ltd
3 Church Street
#10-04 Samsung Hub
Singapore 049483

Library of Congress Control Number: 2012932298

British Library Cataloguing in Publication data

A catalogue record for this book is available from
the British Library

Editor: Michael Carmichael
Editorial assistant: Alana Clogan
Production editor: Vanessa Harwood
Copyeditor: Neville Hankins
Proofreader: Derek Markham
Indexer: Caroline Eley
Marketing manager: Alison Borg
Cover design: Wendy Scott
Typeset by: C&M Digitals (P) Ltd
Printed by: India at Replika Press Pvt Ltd

ISBN 978-0-85702-406-0

Contents

1

Introduction

I wrote this volume in the service of two complementary goals. First, I wanted to provide an introduction to the hows and whys of diary-style research for scholars who are interested in conducting research using diary methods. Second, I wanted to provide scholars, who may not be interested in conducting research using diary methods, sufficient background so that they can make sense of articles describing diary research. To accomplish these goals I discuss how to conceptualize and design a diary study, how to conduct a diary study, and how to analyze the data and report the results of these analyses.

Be forewarned, the style of the writing in this volume is not traditionally academic. Although there are a decent number of references, I have written the volume in a style that resembles what I might say to a colleague as we are discussing a study. I have been conducting diary research for close to 40 years, and, during this time, I would like to think that I have accumulated what would be considered a decent amount of experience. One reason I wrote this volume was to share this experience with a wider audience than the colleagues with whom I have worked. At times, I make recommendations based primarily upon my experience or my general impression of the state of affairs. This is because, for many issues, little if any formal research has been done. As a matter of convenience, many of the examples I use or discuss in more detail are from research I have conducted or with which I have been involved in some way. I did this because I am more familiar with these studies, not because I think they are better than studies conducted by other researchers.

In this volume, I focus on the technology of diary studies: how to design them; how to conduct them; and perhaps most important (and nearest and dearest to my heart), how to analyze the data produced in a diary study. I spend relatively more time on data analysis because I think it is the weakest link in the present chain of scientific inquiry. Although designing and conducting a diary style requires being sensitive to different aspects of a study than is the case for survey and experimental studies, designing and conducting diary studies has much in common with designing and conducting studies using other methods. For example, regardless of how data are collected, self-report items need to be written unambiguously, using language that is appropriate for the participant population.

In contrast, analyzing the data collected in a diary study requires methods other than the variants of ANOVA and regression that are typically used to analyze the data from survey and experimental studies. Although I discuss other options, most diary studies are probably best conceptualized as some type of multilevel data structure in which diary entries/records are treated as nested within persons. Unfortunately, many researchers are unfamiliar with how to conceptualize relationships within the multilevel context and are unfamiliar with conducting multilevel analyses. Given this, I thought a specific focus on how to analyze the data produced by diary studies was needed.

Why diaries instead of other methods?

Before going further, I should probably describe what a diary is and what is meant by the term "diary method." It appears that the English word "diary" is based on the Latin *diarium*, which referred to a daily allowance of food or pay. By the early seventeenth century, the word "diary" had taken on its present meaning of some type of daily record of events maintained and updated by an individual. Although, technically speaking, diaries are a type of daily record, diaries as discussed herein do not need to use the day as an organizing unit. For now, it will suffice to note that personality and social psychologists tend to use diaries with two different types of organizing units. In some studies, people keep a diary that is organized in terms of a type of event. Every time a certain type of event occurs, a diary record is created. In other studies, people keep a diary that is organized in terms of time. Every time a certain amount of time passes (which could, but does not have to be, a day), a diary record is created. I discuss these techniques in detail later.

What these techniques have in common is the fact that an individual provides a description of his or her life on some type of regular basis. In fact, diary research is sometimes described as a type of "intensive repeated measures" design because repeated measures are collected on the same person in what some think of as intensively. You will also see the term "experience sampling" because, in some studies, samples of people's experiences are examined. This is often abbreviated ESM (Experience Sampling Method). Other terms you may see include "ecological momentary assessment" (EMA), a term that is used frequently in the health sciences. Each of these terms has been used to refer to different types of diaries.

Importantly, for the types of diary methods I discuss in this volume, data are collected "in vivo," in the course of people's everyday lives. The focus of most diary studies is not on the dramatic or the unusual aspects of a person's life. Rather, diary studies tend to concern the natural ebb and flow of a person's life, which invariably contains a mixture of the dramatic and the mundane. The value of collecting data in vivo is described in detail by Reis (2012). These advantages include the realism of the settings and contexts within which phenomena are studied and the inclusion of the mundane and *apparently* unimportant aspects of life. As I discuss later, maintaining a diary should not interfere with a person's life. To the extent that it does, maintaining a diary destroys the very thing it is designed to study.

Fair enough, but why not study everyday life (or everyday behaviors) in the laboratory? For many social and personality psychologists, perhaps a bit more for social psychologists, the control and resulting clarity of inference provided by laboratory methods is very attractive. Independent variables can be manipulated, extraneous situational factors can be controlled or eliminated, and causal relationships can be isolated and decomposed. For many researchers, whatever loss of external validity occurs when using laboratory methods is more than offset by the gains in internal validity such methods provide.

Such a calculus has been, and remains, attractive. Nevertheless, by their very nature, laboratory methods are limited in important ways. Some phenomena simply cannot be studied in the laboratory because they cannot exist or be created within the controlled, artificial environment of the lab. Although we can induce feelings of sadness in people, we cannot make them depressed. Similarly, although we can create positive interpersonal bonds, we cannot make people fall in love. Anyone who has been depressed or in love can readily and easily recognize the qualitative differences between these in vivo experiences versus the fleeting states of mind that are created in most experiments.

Even if we could create such states of mind in controlled settings, some phenomena of interest to social and personality psychologists are destroyed when they are controlled. The individuals with whom someone affiliates and how often these people are seen cannot be studied in a controlled setting. Similarly, the types of situations people chose (or find themselves in) and how they react to these situational influences cannot be studied in the lab. Certainly, we can study such topics in the lab in a limited way. We can provide people the opportunity to select others with whom they will interact or to select situations and see how they respond, but it is difficult to imagine that the choices that can be made available in a lab setting can represent the range of options in people's real lives.

Okay, but: "Why do data need to be collected every day or a few times each day? Why not give people a single questionnaire asking them what happened during some period of time such as a week?" The answer is clear. The repeated measures collected in diary studies provide more accurate descriptions of everyday experience than those obtained from single assessment questionnaires that often ask respondents to recall events, thoughts, and feelings over lengthy, sometimes unspecified periods of time. Such vagueness is prone to all sorts of memory biases.

Although there are various lists of why such retrospection is bad (or, more charitably, is subject to error), I think the summary provided by Reis and Gable (2000) does a good job of capturing the important points. I summarize these below, and I add one more point that builds on these. The common theme to these specific problems is perhaps best summarized by the Chinese proverb: "The faintest ink is more powerful than the strongest memory." This proverb also reflects the considerable research demonstrating that memory (retrospection) is a constructive process. The eye is not a camera, and the ear is not a tape recorder. When we remember, we create memories as much, and perhaps more, than we recall memories. In terms of providing descriptions of what has occurred, the longer the time between the event and the description, the more extraneous factors (factors not related to the event itself) can influence the description.

1 *Recency* – Recent experiences are recalled better than temporally distant ones. Moreover, whatever occurs between an experience and the report of that experience is likely to influence the report. The longer the time between an experience and the report of that experience, the greater the opportunity there is for intervening events to influence the report. Such influences may be particularly important when individuals are describing separate experiences of the same type, such as a series of social interactions with the same person. An interaction I just had with a friend of mine may influence my recollection of the interactions I had with him during the past week.

2 *Salience* – More distinctive, important, or personally relevant experiences are recalled better than common or mundane experiences. In addition, more distinctive, important or personally relevant experiences are likely to influence reports of more mundane experiences. Such possibilities are particularly important when considering the relative influence of positive and negative experiences. Considerable research indicates that negative stimuli are more salient than positive stimuli. An argument with a friend or a bad day at work may be remembered better than a pleasant interaction of a normal day at work. In addition, important experiences are likely to influence reports of less important experiences, creating a sort of global report that may not reflect the nature of less important experiences or how people felt or thought during those experiences. An argument with a friend may influence my description of other, less dramatic interactions I had with him. An unusually bad day at work may lead me to think about other days differently.

3 *Sense-making* – Individuals have various implicit theories and they hold various stereotypes, and these implicit theories and stereotypes help people organize reality. As a result, individuals tend to reconstruct their recollections in terms of their general beliefs, often overriding reactions they would have provided at the time they experienced something. As the time between an experience and a report increases and as the number of reports increases, the distinctiveness of each experience decreases. As the distinctiveness of an experience per se decreases, the influence of implicit theories and stereotypes on reports of that experience is likely to increase.

4 *Present state of mind* – Individuals' present or immediate state of mind such as moods or attitudes can influence memories, including reports of previous experiences. Such influences can take two forms. Present states of mind may influence the specific experiences that are recalled. For example, when in a good mood, people may be more likely to recall positive experiences, whereas when they are in

a bad mood they may be more likely to recall negative experiences. Present states of mind may also influence reports of experiences per se. For someone who holds strong negative attitudes about a certain ethnic group, a retrospective report about an interethnic interaction may be more negative than a report that is provided more contemporaneously.

5 *Making distinctions* – As discussed by Nezlek and Schaafsma (2010), compared to reports generated in diary studies, retrospective reports tend to reflect more strongly the operation of a single (often, hedonic) dimension. When thinking about multiple experiences in the perhaps distant past, people are less likely to make distinctions among different aspects of those experiences compared to the distinctions they make when providing more immediate reports. The hedonic (good–bad) dimension seems to be the one that is the most salient across time. The fact that a retrospective report asks people to distinguish different aspects of an experience (e.g., satisfaction with an interaction vs. how influential an individual felt during an interaction) does not mean that people make such distinctions when providing retrospective reports. For the reasons just discussed, when providing retrospective reports, people do not tend to distinguish different aspects of an experience as well as when they are making a contemporaneous report. For example, relationships (e.g., correlations) between different evaluations tend to be stronger for retrospective reports than they are for contemporaneous reports.

All of this is not to say that single assessment, retrospective measures are not valuable. If I ask you how your life was last week and you reply "Miserable," that is meaningful and potentially valuable in terms of understanding your life. On the other hand, it may not be a good measure of how you felt each day of last week. On six of those seven days you may have felt fine, but on the last day of the week something terrible happened, which colored your impression of the other days. Perhaps more important, it may also be that some type of measure based on individual reports from all seven days provides a more useful measure (in terms of relationships with other criteria) than the single assessment, global retrospective report.

Although both laboratory-based studies and single assessment surveys are limited in important ways, I have no desire to denigrate or criticize these methods per se. They are valid and informative ways of understanding the human condition. In this volume, I will be describing how to design and conduct diary studies and how to analyze the data they produce without constantly comparing diary and other methods mano-a-mano.

Levels of analysis

In addition to providing more ecologically valid and accurate descriptions of people's lives than lab and survey methods, diary methods also provide a better basis for examining psychological phenomena at different levels of analysis.

When describing diary studies, the phrase "levels of analysis" refers to two mutually defining aspects of the data collected in a study, the technical and the conceptual. Moreover, for most diary studies, there are two levels of analysis, the person level and the diary level. There can be more than two levels, and I discuss such possibilities later.

Technically speaking, level of analysis refers to the focus of the measures that are collected in a study. Person-level measures include those that describe something about a person that is presumed not to vary over the course of a study, such as an individual's sex and personality traits. In contrast, diary-level measures include those that describe something about a diary entry (or record – the target of the diary per se), and diary level measures are presumed to vary across the diary entries for individuals. A measure of mood that is collected every day is a prototypical diary-level measure. I discuss person- and diary-level measures later in separate sections.

Conceptually speaking, level of analysis refers to the level at which a phenomenon (including relationships between constructs) is thought to reside. This also includes the type or nature of the processes that relationships between measures are meant to represent. Relationships at the person level involve person-level measures, and they concern person-level processes. For example, the relationship between trait self-esteem and trait anxiety indicates if people who are more anxious tend to have a lower sense of self-worth compared to individuals who are less anxious. In contrast, relationships at the diary level involve diary-level measures, and they concern diary-level or within-person processes. For example, the relationship between a daily measure of mood and a daily measure of stress indicates if people's mood is poorer on days when they experience more stress than on days when they experience less stress.

It is critical to keep in mind that relationships at these two levels of analysis are both technically and conceptually distinct. Technically, as I explain later, relationships between two constructs measured at the person level are mathematically unrelated to relationships between these same two constructs measured at the diary (or within-person) level (Nezlek, 2001). Perhaps more important, conceptually, relationships at the two levels of analysis may represent different psychological phenomena (Affleck, Zautra, Tennen, & Armeli, 1999).

In diary studies, multiple observations are collected for each person, providing a basis for analyzing within-person relationships (diary-level relationships). Although it is theoretically possible, in the lab, it is difficult to collect the data that are needed to provide good estimates of within-person relationships such as that between stress and anxiety. How many different experimental conditions can people experience before the quality of the data they provide becomes questionable? Although such repeated measures could be asked in a survey, how well can people provide retrospective accounts of events and internal states for a sufficient number of occasions to provide a basis to estimate within-person relationships?

Whatever shortcomings diary studies have, it seems that they provide the best opportunity to examine within-person processes. Moreover, they can do so in a way that maximizes the ecological validity of the study. Truly, they can study "life as it is lived" (Bolger, Davis, & Rafaeli, 2003).

Note that, in the literature, person level is sometimes referred to as "between person" to provide a more fitting complement to "within person." Throughout this volume, I will use person level and between person interchangeably, and I will use diary level and within person interchangeably.

Does keeping a diary per se influence what a person reports?

It appears that the multiple real-world observations collected in diary studies can provide unique advantages compared to other methods. If so, we should consider the potential disadvantages of asking people to answer the same questions on a repeated basis. One possible disadvantage is that providing responses in such a fashion might influence what people report. Such an influence could concern responses per se. Do people tend to answer questions differently at the end (or middle) of a diary than they do at the beginning? Do they become sensitized to certain events and conditions and increase the number of events they describe over time? Or, do they become desensitized, bored, or tired, and describe fewer events in less detail over time? Alternatively, and perhaps more fundamental, does keeping a diary change a person's life, aside from what they report about it? For example, if I record all my social interactions, do I change with whom I interact or how I think about my interactions as I see as an objective description of my social life developing before my eyes?

For the most part, researchers have assumed that diaries are non-reactive in both senses of the term as described above, and there is some research supporting such an assumption. Although self-reports of reactivity do not constitute a case on their own, in post-study interviews with participants in studies using the Rochester Interaction Record, of which I have been part, participants have rarely reported any sort of meaningful change as a result of maintaining the record. Some have reported an increased awareness of what they were doing: for example, "I never realized how much time I spent with the same group of people." Such individuals did not report, however, that they changed their behavior as a result of this awareness. Similarly, I have compared the first and second halves of the data I have collected in some of my daily diary studies (usually a week for each half). Although I have found differences between the halves in means of some measures, these differences were quite small, and there were no differences in within-person covariances between measures, and such covariances were the focus of my hypotheses.

Moreover, in a series of studies discussed by Hufford (2007), researchers did not find any evidence for reactivity. Admittedly, these studies did not concern all types of diaries focusing on a wide range of topics. They primarily concerned momentary assessment studies of patient-reported outcomes such as pain. Nevertheless, to my knowledge, no one has demonstrated that maintaining (per se) the types of diaries that are discussed in this book meaningfully changes the behaviors of the diary keeper. For a more thorough discussion of this topic (that reaches a similar conclusion) see Barta, Tennen, and Litt (2012). Barta et al. also suggest, however, that not enough is known about reactivity because it has not been studied that carefully and that more research is needed before we can safely assume that maintaining a diary does not lead to systematic changes in the behaviors of the diary keepers.

Nevertheless, some research suggests that under some circumstances, maintaining a diary may lead to changes in those who are maintaining it. As might be expected, much of this research has been conducted by researchers with a clinical interest or focus; however, the issues this research raises and addresses may be relevant to the interests of some social and personality psychologists. As discussed by Carter, Day, Cinciripini, and Wetter (2007), maintaining a diary "increases the patient's awareness of the frequency, patterns, and circumstances attendant to a target behavior" (p. 293). They further discussed how the feedback provided by a diary may reduce undesirable behaviors and increase desirable behaviors. Note that they discuss "patients," and mention "target behaviors."

What is important to note about the type of research discussed by Carter et al. is that invariably the diary keepers in such studies had goals of some kind. They were patients, under care, and they (presumably) wanted to make some type of change in their behavior or they wanted to maintain some type of change they had made. There were explicitly desirable behaviors such as exercise or compliance with medication protocols, and there were explicitly undesirable behaviors such as smoking or eating too much fat.

In contrast, in many (or perhaps most, or virtually all) diary studies conducted by personality and social psychologists there are no explicitly desirable and undesirable behaviors. Quite the opposite. Researchers typically make it clear to participants that there are no desirable or undesirable behaviors. Participants are told that the researchers are simply interested in their daily life per se. In fact, to the extent possible without creating issues about reactivity, participants are often reminded that they should not change their behaviors or routines because they are maintaining the diary.

So, the available evidence appears to suggest that when people maintain a diary without an explicit goal or end state in mind, maintaining a diary does not seem to have a meaningful influence on their thoughts, feelings, or behaviors. In contrast, diaries can be considered as a type of intervention when there is some type of desired goal or end state in the mind of the participant.

Additional resources

Regardless of your level of familiarity with diary research, you may find the following sources helpful. This list is not meant to be complete, although the articles and chapters do cover most of the major issues. Moreover, for readers who are not familiar with diary-style research or certain aspects of such research, these are "good places to start." I have omitted some earlier citations whose content or contributions were either dated or covered in more recent citations. Later, I present a similar list of sources for data analysis.

- Wheeler and Reis (1991) – A discussion of the relative advantages and disadvantages of different data collection protocols.
- Affleck, Zautra, Tennen, and Armeli (1999) – A discussion/explanation of why it is important to distinguish relationships at different levels of analysis, specifically between person vs. within person.
- Gable and Reis (1999) – A review of using within-person designs (mainly diary methods) to study personal relationships.
- Reis and Gable (2000) – A review of methods of studying everyday experience.
- Bolger, Davis, and Rafaeli (2003) – A review of various aspects of diary research with a focus on methods and analytic techniques.
- Stone, Shiffman, Atienza, and Nebeling (2007a) – A review of the development of ecological momentary assessment (EMA) techniques in the health sciences, including a rationale for them.
- Nezlek and Schaafsma (2010) – A discussion of the advantages of using diary style methods to study interethnic contact.
- Reis (2012) – A broad overview and rationale for using diary-style methods.

In addition, a forthcoming handbook, edited by Mehl and Conner (2012), has chapters concerning various aspects of diary-style research. For those interested in EMA with a focus on applications in health I recommend Stone, Shiffman, Atienza, and Nebeling (2007b), an edited volume based on a 2003 meeting convened by the US National Cancer Institute.

The important advantage of the present volume over other sources (at least for personality and social psychologists) is that I discuss aspects of diary research in terms that are particularly relevant to personality and social psychologists and do so in greater depth and detail than is available elsewhere (with all modesty). Moreover, in this volume, discussions of design, analysis, and reporting issues are fully integrated. Finally, and consistent with the focus of the series of which this volume is a part, I discuss topics in a fashion that makes them accessible to the non-expert.

2

Designing a study

When designing a diary-style study, the most important consideration should be the question motivating the study, and the fact that some type of diary method is the best or only way to study the topic in which you are interested. For example, assume you are interested in the extent to which people interact with a small group of close friends versus a larger group of perhaps not so close friends. Although you could study this with some type of single assessment (one-shot) questionnaire, as discussed previously, such broadly focused retrospective measures are fraught with problems. A diary method is likely to provide data that are less influenced by the biases inherent in retrospective measures, which in turn will provide a basis for more accurate conclusions.

The phrase "diary method" is somewhat ambiguous, and the term has been applied to all sorts of ways of collecting data. Regardless, as discussed in the Introduction, the common element these techniques have is that participants provide descriptions of their daily lives on some type of regular basis. In terms of designing a diary study, I will start by describing what I consider to be the essential characteristic of a diary study as discussed by Wheeler and Reis (1991) – the basis on which data are collected or on which records are generated. This basis is the defining characteristic of what I will refer to as the *data collection protocol* – the general framework of a study.

Wheeler and Reis distinguished three different types of diaries. One was *event contingent*. In an event contingent study, the occurrence of a specific type of event such as a social interaction triggers data collection. Using some type of fixed format form, participants describe all the events that have occurred since the last time they provided data. A second data collection protocol was *interval contingent*. In an interval contingent study, the passage of a specific, fixed amount of time (an interval) triggers data collection. For example, an individual might provide data at the end of each day, or at regular intervals during each day (e.g., noon, 6pm, and before going to bed). A third data collection protocol was *signal contingent*. In a signal contingent study, data are collected in response to some type of signal, usually at randomly spaced intervals. A good example of this is the "beeper" studies of Csikszentmihalyi and colleagues (e.g., Csikszentmihalyi & Larson, 1987). People wear a wristwatch that beeps, and when it does, they provide data. Before discussing how to select the data collection protocol that is best suited to answer different types of questions, I will briefly describe the different protocols.

Event contingent studies

In event contingent studies, participants use some type of structured form to describe the event that is the focus of the study. In the best of all possible worlds, they complete a form immediately after a target event has ended – one form for each event. This reduces the types of biases and errors that can occur when people retrospect about events in the perhaps distant past. In reality, in many studies, participants update their diaries a few times each day, assuming that the event in question occurs more than once each day.

Regardless, the most important, critical, and essential aspect of an event contingent study is defining the event unambiguously. Participants need to know what constitutes (and what does not constitute) the event they should be describing. For more objective (externally viewable) events, you will probably need to supply less detail than you will for events that are more subjective. Although a certain amount of individual differences in interpretation of what constitutes an event is inevitable, your goal is to minimize the influence of such differences in your study.

Following my work developing what has come to be known as the Rochester Interaction Record (Wheeler & Nezlek, 1977), most of the research I have conducted that has used an event contingent protocol has concerned social interaction. The definition is straightforward and goes something like this: "an interaction is an encounter with one or more other people in which the participants attend to one another and adjust their behavior in response to one another." This definition follows Goffman's (1971) concept of a "social with." Fortunately, virtually all participants (of various types) have had little, if any, difficulty understanding what constitutes a social interaction. Participants describe all the social interactions they have that last 10 minutes or longer. Participants in my social interaction studies have updated their diaries just under twice per day. I have included an appendix, "Sample social interaction diary instructions," that contains examples of instructions I have used.

Nevertheless, various other types of events can and have been studied. For example, Wheeler and Miyake (1992) used social comparison as an event, Nezlek, Wesselman, Williams, and Wheeler (in press) used being ostracized, Smith, Nezlek, Webster, and Paddock (2007) used sexual interactions as the defining event, and DePaulo, Kashy, Kirekndol, Wyer, and Epstein (1996) studied lies. Moreover, if you read the methods sections of these papers, you will see that meaningful attention was paid to defining the event in question. By the way, this list of types of events is not meant to be exhaustive (in the slightest), simply illustrative.

The data participants describe regarding each event typically concern two different aspects of the event. One is what I will call "structural or quantitative" aspects – what happened or what was occurring, where and when the event occurred, the others who were present, and so forth. Questions can also concern what I refer to as "qualitative" aspects of the event, how people felt, reacted to something, perceived an event, and so forth. These two types of data provide the basis for descriptive statistics about the events per se, and they provide a basis to compare different subtypes of events. Later in the section on data analysis, I describe some different ways this might be done. For example, in a social interaction diary study, a researcher might be interested in differences between interactions that involve close friends and those that do not.

The specific data you request about each event will vary as a function of the focus of the study and your hypotheses of interest. It is important that you collect the data that will be needed to answer questions reviewers and readers may have about the nature of the events that participants described. For example, if you are studying arguments, it would seem to be critical to know with whom the argument occurred, what the source of disagreement was, and so forth. Keep in mind that in an event contingent study, the specific types of events people experience and describe may vary systematically (non-randomly) across persons, an issue I address later in a section on non-random sampling.

Interval and signal contingent studies

I will introduce interval and signal contingent studies together because they have much in common. In both types of studies, participants provide data at specific points in time. In an interval contingent study, when participants provide data is fixed and consistent across participants. A common protocol is a study in which participants provide data every day, typically at the end of the day. Common variations request data two or three times per day. There is no true limit to the number of times per day data can be collected, although there are practical considerations that I discuss later.

In a signal contingent study, participants provide data when they are signaled, typically at random intervals. One of the rationales for the random signaling is that it reduces the influence of anticipation on participants' responses. In most signal contingent studies, the number of times a participant is signaled each day (observations) is constant across participants, but the specific times individual participants are asked to provide data vary. Although the interval between adjacent observations varies, there may be maximum intervals, minimum intervals, and an average interval that is scheduled to be the same across participants. For example, a signal contingent protocol might request eight observations each day, with a minimum of 20 minutes and a maximum of 120 minutes between each observation. Another method involves dividing a day into segments (e.g., 90 minutes each), and sending a signal at a random time within each of these segments.

When considering some type of interval or signal contingent protocol, the critical question concerns the temporal nature of the phenomenon in which you are interested. For example, are the within-person relationships in which you are interested entities that can be reasonably conceptualized as existing at the day level, or is a more fine-grained level of analysis necessary? If the phenomenon is more fine grained, a more intensive data collection protocol may be required (e.g., multiple measures each day).

Obtaining multiple measures within a longer unit of time can be done by obtaining multiple reports within a unit of time (e.g., multiple reports every day) or by obtaining measures describing discrete periods of time simultaneously. Good examples of the former are beeper-style studies. In such studies, people are typically asked to describe what is going on at a specific time. A good example of the latter is an experience sampling study of the duration of emotional experience, Verduyn, Delvaux, Van Coillie, Tuerlinckx, and Van Mechelen (2007). At the end of each day, participants used a form that allowed them to describe their emotional experiences in 15-minute intervals.

In terms of understanding within-person covariation (an important focus of diary research), it is essential to have a clear conceptualization of the level of analysis at which the phenomena reside. As discussed later in the section on nesting and levels of analysis, the structure of the data needs to correspond to this conceptualization. If the covariation in which you are interested resides at the within-day level, you will need to collect data multiple times each day. Moreover, if you think that these within-day relationships vary as a function of some day-level characteristic, you will need to sample enough days to model this variability.

Although it is difficult to generalize broadly across the large number of studies that have been done using these methods, with this caveat in mind, I offer the following general conclusions. In most interval and signal contingent studies, participants answer a series of structured, close-ended, questions, typically the same questions each time they provide a report. Open-ended responses are certainly possible, but keep in mind that they need to be coded later. Although some researchers vary the order in which questions are asked across occasions, most do not. Data can be collected using pencil and paper methods, but, increasingly, researchers are collecting data electronically. As discussed later, electronic data collection provides date and time stamps, which can be particularly important when evaluating participants' compliance with signal and interval contingent protocols. Moreover, and particularly for signal contingent protocols, the device that emits the signal that triggers data collection is also being used to collect the data.

Depending upon the interval between observations, interval contingent studies tend to rely upon reports that are somewhat retrospective. For example, if data are collected at the end of a day, individuals are usually asked to provide some type of description of how they felt that day, what happened during the day, and so forth. Even if the interval is less than a full day (e.g., three observations per day), reports still tend to be somewhat retrospective. For example, at noon, people might be asked to describe how they felt that morning. Some find even this amount of retrospection troubling, but daily reports are accepted as valid by many different groups of researchers.

In contrast, in signal contingent studies, the focus of the questions tends to be more immediate. How are you feeling *now*? What is going on around you *now*? A more retrospective focus is possible (e.g., what has happened since the last report?), but in signal contingent studies the tendency is for items to focus on the immediate present.

In addition to a difference in temporal focus, interval and signal contingent protocols tend to differ in terms of the amount of information that is requested on each measurement occasion. As a guiding principle, data collection should not change people's lives; it should simply be part of their lives for the time of the study. Signal contingent studies typically request multiple reports each day, and these reports are typically provided in the midst of people's lives. People get beeped and provide a report soon thereafter. This combination makes it difficult to request much information at each report. Data collection typically takes less than a minute.

In contrast, in interval contingent studies, typically, participants set aside some time each day to provide their reports. The amount of time this takes varies widely, but it can be as much as 5 or even 10 minutes. Such a procedure provides the opportunity to collect meaningfully more data on each occasion than is collected in a signal contingent study. Nonetheless, as I discuss later, in the section on intensity of data collection, you need to be mindful of the cumulative demands a data collection protocol has on participants.

Exactly what is measured on each occasion in interval and signal contingent studies will vary as a function of the questions of interest. Similar to event contingent studies, the data collected at each observation can concern structural characteristics (e.g., situational features, who was present) and internal states. Much of the research using these two protocols has focused on emotion or affect, but there is no technical reason for such a focus, and later, in the section on diary-level measures, I discuss various possibilities.

Studies using integrated interval and event contingent protocols

Although such studies are not common, interval and event contingent protocols can be combined in a single study. For example, participants can complete an end-of-day record (interval contingent) while providing descriptions of the instances of some type of an event that occurred each day (event contingent). This was done by Mohr, Armeli, Tennen, Carney, Affleck, and Hromi (2001). In this study, they used an event contingent protocol to collect data about alcohol consumption. Every time a participant had a drink, he or she provided a description of the event. These descriptions included amount, circumstances, and so forth. These reports were combined with data collected using an interval contingent protocol, a daily diary. At the end of each day, participants provided data describing the negative and positive interpersonal exchanges they had that day. The primary analyses focused on the relationships between consumption (amount, circumstances, etc.) and interpersonal exchanges.

I have conducted an integrated study (data not yet fully analyzed) and in this study participants maintained a social interaction diary (a variant of the Rochester Interaction Record (RIR)), and they provided end-of-day reports. I must caution researchers that such studies can be very demanding on participants. Preliminary analyses of the data collected in my study have suggested a somewhat higher "bad data" rate than is typical, not fatally higher, but higher nonetheless. In combination, the two tasks probably pushed participants to their limit. The next time I do such a study, I will reduce the demand generated by both components.

As described, in the Mohr et al. study, it seems that the combined protocol they used was not that demanding. Events (drinks) were recorded using an electronic device, and the end-of-day report was not very long. Compliance with protocol in their study was uniformly good.

I mention how demanding a protocol is because I think researchers often forget just how much work it is for participants to provide data every day, and in the case of the examples I just discussed, two types of data every day. As scholars, we want to know everything, and our passion may blind us to the realities of the demands of people's lives. Providing data in a study should be "the tail" not "the dog" in people's lives. One way to ensure this is to pretest methods and determine how demanding a protocol will be. A bit of advice – when pretesting, use someone other than your best friends or favorite students.

What can be studied using a diary method?

The topics that can be studied using diary methods are limited only by the creativity of the researchers who are interested in using them. Truly, the sky is the limit. Noting this, just as when designing a study using another method, researchers need to have a clear idea of what they want to know when designing a diary study. It can be tempting simply to collect a bunch of data and see where they take you, but without any conceptual or theoretical guidance you can wind up with a lot of data that may very well end up saying nothing.

As discussed in the previous chapter, diary studies can be conducted simply to determine how often something happens or occurs. If this is the primary focus, researchers need to be particularly careful about the samples they study. If I want to know how often people get drunk, I will probably overestimate the average for the general population if I study a sample of collegians using some type of diary that collects reports about whether participants drank too much each day. Although I am dubious about how truly generalizable to the general population lab-based studies of cognitive processes using sophomores might be, such generalizability is probably easier to defend than generalizing about alcohol consumption. In many respects, sophomores may not think differently than the general population, or, at the least, it may seem reasonable to assume that they do not differ in ways that are meaningful to the theories being examined.

Diary studies can also be used to study more process-like phenomena such as reactions to stress. Such studies will more than likely focus on some type of within-person process (e.g., changes in mood or self-evaluation as a function of stressful events) and can focus on between-person differences in such within-person relationships. Although such studies are not immune from considerations of representativeness, the fact that they are studying process probably reduces (in the minds of many) concerns about generalizability.

Participant commitment

By their nature, diary studies tend to require more of a commitment on the part of participants than is required of participants in studies using other methods. In survey-based studies, participants will answer a set of questions once, perhaps two or three times if part of a panel, but the time that is needed to do this is relatively short. Moreover, contact between participants and researchers is typically initiated by the researcher. Similarly, in a lab study, participants do what they are told to do (more or less), and their involvement consists of a session or two, all of which is initiated and controlled by the researcher.

In contrast, in most diary studies, participants are much more "on their own." Yes, they receive instructions from the researchers, yes, they are given instructions and/ or access to a website with instructions, and yes, they may receive reminders and follow-up messages to maximize their adherence to the data collection protocol. But, unless they are in a study in which data are collected automatically (e.g., blood pressure, heart rate, etc., via a device of some kind), they need to take the initiative to provide the data researchers want. Moreover, by intent and design, participants are expected to provide these data far from the watchful eyes of researchers and their assistants. The norms that ensure compliance when responding to a survey administrator and when in the lab are meaningfully less salient when an authority figure is not present than when an authority figure is present (recall Milgram).

The upshot of all this is that diary studies need to be designed with an understanding of what it is realistic to expect of participants, and these expectations need to take into account the life circumstances of the participants. Many researchers are accustomed to dealing with college students who will do just about anything they are asked to do. Students will answer endless series of seemingly repetitive (or actually repetitive) questions and do so over and over again. In contrast, adults living in the community will not, and if researchers use the same protocols for community residents that they use for students one of two things is likely to happen. First, they will have high rates of non-compliance, and, second, the sample of community residents who comply may not be representative of the broader population.

This is not to say that diary studies cannot involve participants other than compliant collegians. Many diary studies have studied non-collegians with considerable success. Rather, I mention this to caution researchers, who are accustomed to studying collegians, about problems they may have if they get off campus. Moreover, although these are problems that are less likely to occur with non-diary methods than they are with diary methods, they are problems that can be minimized by pretesting methods to determine how easy it will be for participants to comply with a data collection protocol.

Regardless of the specific participant population, researchers need to recognize that the success of a study depends upon the willingness of participants to comply with the data collection protocol. In my social interaction diary research, I have tried to do this by telling participants that they are co-investigators and that it would be impossible to study naturally occurring social interaction using other methods – both of which are true. Also, in the introductory session to a study, I go through the data collection protocol with participants to demonstrate that completing the forms does not take longer than the five or so minutes I tell them it will take.

Researchers need to determine what it will take to secure the cooperation of their participants. Researchers often use reminder messages (email, text, phone, whatever is appropriate) to ensure that participants comply with instructions. One of the advantages of online data collection is the ability to monitor participant compliance. Participants who have not complied with protocols can be asked why. My experience has been that once participants start a study and provide a day or two of data, they tend to "stick with it" and continue until the study is over. Occasionally, we have participants who provide more days than is requested. Some enjoy it, some are eager to please or to ensure that they have met a requirement.

Certainly, financial rewards can be used to increase compliance (if not commitment per se); however, depending upon how one interprets ethical considerations, it may not be practical to withhold financial rewards (or other rewards such as research participation credits) as a function of how fully or how well participants have complied with a data collection protocol. One possibility I have considered is to recruit individuals from an organization of some kind and create a reward structure in which the organization gets a reward for an individual's participation. In this way, the individual is not working for him- or herself, and there is the additional pressure on the individual to participate for the benefit of the organization.

Nonetheless, as discussed later in the chapter on data preparation, deleting some records for some participants and all the data for some participants is de rigueur. In all the studies I have conducted, some records (e.g., days of data) were deleted for some participants, and all of the data of some participants were deleted. Compliance is unlikely to be perfect, but the important issue is to ensure that compliance is good enough to ensure the representativeness of the data that are provided.

Combining type of diary, length of study, and frequency/intensity of data collection

When designing a diary study, there are four important considerations: the type of diary people will be keeping; how long you want people to maintain the diary; the frequency with which people will be providing data; and how much information you will obtain on each measurement occasion.

Deciding what type of diary to use should be determined by the substantive questions at hand. If you are interested in studying some type of definable event, such as social interactions, arguments, or internal states of some kind, an event contingent protocol is probably best. In contrast, if you are interested in within-person relationships between a psychological state and an external condition (e.g., anxiety and stressful events) or the relationship between two psychological states (e.g., mood and self-esteem), some type of interval or signal contingent protocol is probably best.

If you are thinking about using a signal contingent protocol to study a specific occurrence or state, be certain to take into account how frequently that occurrence or state occurs. As I discussed earlier, in most signal contingent protocols, participants answer questions about their immediate circumstances and feelings. What percentage of moments in a waking day does the target event or state exist? If the answer is very little, unless you request data very frequently you may not capture enough instances of the event or state to provide a basis for analyses.

Event contingent protocols have the advantage of providing detailed descriptions of the focal event, but they tend not to provide much information about the broader context within which the event is occurring. In contrast, signal and interval contingent protocols do not provide much information about specific occurrences, but they can provide detailed descriptions of changes in people's lives. If you are uncertain about the type of protocol that you should use, consult the existing literature to see what others have done. Although you may not find a study that has focused on your specific topic, you may find studies that have examined questions that are *structurally* similar to yours. In this instance, the term "structurally" refers to the nature of the relationships being examined.

Another factor to consider is the frequency with which you expect or want participants to provide data. For event contingent protocols, you should be certain that participants provide reports no more than a few hours after the event has occurred. The less time that elapses, the better. It is probably unreasonable to expect people to stop their lives to complete a diary form, but you should impress upon them the importance of updating their diaries as frequently as possible. As discussed later in the chapter on data preparation, in my social interaction diary research, we have allowed "next day" reports, but only up to a certain time, typically 10am. For event contingent studies, how often people provide data is not a concern per se. More occasions are more desirable because more frequent reporting reduces the influence on reports of events and states of mind that are not part of the target event itself.

In contrast, for interval and signal contingent studies, when and how often people provide data is foundational. Although some leeway in terms of "response windows" is typically allowed, participants need to respond at the specified intervals to provide the data needed for the analyses. For example, if you are studying daily-level phenomena, people need to provide data once a day, every day, at the end of the day (or at the same time each day).

Noting this, the question remains: How often should data be collected? If you are interested in within-day effects (e.g., mornings vs. evenings), you will need to collect data that will allow you to compare morning and evenings (e.g., twice a day). Moreover, as discussed previously (and later in the section on nesting and levels), if you are collecting multiple observations per day (as in most signal contingent studies), you may need to conceptualize your design in terms of a within-day model. Otherwise, you may confound between- and within-day variances.

In terms of length of study and intensity of data collection, the following guidelines may be helpful: (1) the less frequently the entity that is the focus of your study occurs, the longer your study will need to be; and (2) the more frequently you request information, the less information you can request on each occasion.

Although various factors need to be taken into account when deciding how long a study should last, the most important is the absolute frequency of the activity, state, what-have-you, that is the focus of the study. Does the study concern something that happens every day, once a week, once a month, and so forth? As the focus of a study becomes less frequent, the need to use a diary method (or the benefits of using a diary method compared to other methods) decreases. For example, in an area in which crime is uncommon (e.g., less often than once a month), it makes little sense to study reactions to crime by asking people to maintain a daily diary and then compare their moods on days on which a crime occurred to moods on days on which a crime did not occur. In contrast, if crime occurs frequently, then it makes more sense to do so.

I know of no hard and fast rule regarding how to determine the length of a study as a function of how often a target event or situation occurs. Nevertheless, researchers need to recognize that diary entries represent a sampling of sorts. To avoid the influence of idiosyncratic factors that can occur when samples are small, a study needs to be long enough to ensure that the sample of the target phenomena is large enough to provide a basis for inference. Some of the advantages of diary techniques are due to the repeated measures they produce. If participants provide data describing only one or two instances of some phenomenon, the advantages of collecting repeated measures are lost. When only one or two instances of a target phenomenon are captured, the advantages that are the result of having participants provide reactions, descriptions, and so forth closer to the phenomenon (versus temporally distant) will still hold, but they may not offset the expense of conducting a diary study. Phenomena that occur infrequently might be better studied by some type of cross-sectional study.

Another factor to consider when designing a study is the likely motivation and commitment of the participants. Diary studies typically require participants to provide data at least once a day (if not more frequently) for some extended period (i.e., more than 1–2 days). This means that participants need to be more committed to a diary study than is required of individuals for whom participation is more passive, such as taking a survey. Although I briefly described how I have tried to increase participants' commitment, exactly how this can be accomplished will vary from situation to situation.

In terms of length of studies per se, given that the day and the week are near universal ways of organizing time, I plan the length of studies using these as organizing themes. For most studies, I recommend two weeks because this minimizes the effects that idiosyncratic weeks may have on the results. An individual may have a strange or odd week, but people are unlikely to have two odd weeks in a row (hence the adjective odd). This is a simple application of basic sampling theory – having more observations reduces the influence of unusual observations on the results of analyses.

It may be difficult to obtain uniform and consistent compliance for an extended period when data collection protocols are intense (i.e., when they require many responses each day). In such cases, researchers may want to add participants (see next section) to compensate for the reduced number of entries per participant and the increased error variance that tends to accompany fewer observations. If a data collection protocol is sufficiently intense so that compliance for something such as longer than a week is an issue, I recommend making the protocol less intense. Over the years, I have come to believe that less intense protocols provide better data. This is a simple reflection of the fact that an individual's cognitive and temporal resources are limited, and increasing the number of responses necessarily means decreasing the resources available for each response.

Before the advent of electronic data collection, the mechanics of setting up a study and preparing the data for analysis (e.g., transferring data from paper to some type of electronic medium) were cumbersome and time consuming. In such cases, it made more sense to "pack in" as much as possible to a single study. Although organizing a study (e.g., designing materials, recruiting participants) in the contemporary milieu can still take considerable resources and may justify (at least in a researcher's mind) an intense protocol, I recommend entertaining the possibility that "less is more." Fewer items focused on fewer constructs will provide better insights into a phenomenon than a bloated study that tries to "be all things to all people." I discuss this issue later in the next chapter on diary-level measures.

Another aspect of the data collection protocol that needs to be considered is how often participants will be asked to provide data. It is unreasonable to expect people to answer 5 or 10 minutes' worth of questions every hour or even every few hours. They might answer the questions, but frankly I would be concerned about the validity of the data they provide. As I discussed earlier, this is one of the important differences between signal and interval contingent protocols. Most signal contingent protocols request data too frequently to allow participants to provide more than a few responses on each occasion.

In the daily diary studies I have conducted, it usually takes participants less than five minutes to provide the data each day, and this has not proved problematic. In the social interaction diary studies, the amount of time on each occasion is about the same, although participants typically provide data more than once per day. I strongly recommend that you pretest your protocol to determine how long it is likely to take participants to provide the data you request. If you are collecting data multiple times per day, I recommend that you keep it "short and sweet" – under a minute or two. If participants are providing data only once or twice per day, you can certainly extend this to five minutes or so. In general, less is more – less time is better.

Regardless of the specific protocol you use, it is best to minimize the length of time between when something has happened/occurred and when participants provide their reports. The longer the length of time between the two, the more likely it is that unwanted factors will influence people's reports. Nevertheless, reducing this gap needs to be balanced with the realities of participants' lives. Data collection protocols should not interfere with participants' lives.

Also, regardless of the data collection protocol, participants need to know that they should not select certain events or focus on certain times only, unless, of course, this is the focus of the study. In this regard, I am not an advocate of studies that request reports of only important or significant events or times or that limit participants to a fixed number of events per time period. Both types of limits introduce unknown biases into the data.

Finally, irrespective of the data collection protocol, researchers should ensure that the methods they use are appropriate for the participant sample. Will participants comply with the protocol? Do the measures capture the constructs of interest? And most important, how closely does the researchers' conceptualization of the phenomenon under study correspond to participants' conceptualization? When developing a protocol and set of measures, I typically conduct a few focus groups to determine what data should be collected and how they should be collected, and some pretesting follows this.

Thinking about sample sizes and power

The ability to detect relationships within the types of multilevel data structures that most diary studies produce is a function of many factors. As is the case with any analysis, more observations are better than fewer observations, and this applies to both the number of participants and the number of observations (entries, records, etc.) each participant supplies. Nevertheless, there is the "law of diminishing returns," and as discussed above, at some point, researchers need to be wary of the possibility that requesting more data per person will result in the collection of poorer data per person.

When thinking of sample sizes within the multilevel context, researchers need to consider the nature of the relationships their hypotheses or questions of interest concern. As discussed in more detail in various sections below, such hypotheses tend to take four basic forms. Issues of power also arise when different types of analyses are conducted, such as those that estimate measures of instability for individuals. I discuss measures of instability in a separate chapter.

1 Estimating the mean of a diary-level measure, e.g., how anxious do people tend to be?
2 Examining relationships between means of diary-level measures and person-level measures, e.g., is neuroticism related to the daily anxiety a person experiences?
3 Estimating the mean covariance (relationship) between diary-level measures, e.g., what is the mean (typical) diary-level (within-person) relationship between daily anxiety and daily stress?
4 Examining person-level differences in such diary-level (within-person) relationships, e.g., does the relationship between daily anxiety and daily stress vary as a function of neuroticism?

Assuming that the data will be analyzed using some type of multilevel modeling, various standards regarding power analysis have been proposed. A reasonable discussion of some of these various (and somewhat inconsistent) standards can be found in Richter (2006), and I discuss the issue in Nezlek (2011), the volume about multilevel modeling that is part of this series. These recommendations vary so much that they prohibit a tidy summary, although I provide some tentative recommendations in the next section.

The difficulty in providing firm recommendations reflects the fact that power varies as a function of the number of persons, number of diary entries, the size of the fixed effects being examined, and the reliability of the coefficients of interest. When thinking of sample sizes, typically, the primary concerns are within-person relationships and the possible between-person moderators of these within-person relationships. Within the multilevel framework, one of the most important considerations when thinking of such analyses is the reliability of the within-person coefficients, and the reliability of within-person coefficients is a function of the number of observations and the nature of the relationship itself. The less reliable a coefficient is, the more difficult it is to model between-person variability in that coefficient.

Generally, estimates of within-person means are more reliable than estimates of within-person covariances (within-person relationships, also called slopes). This reflects the psychometric reality that the reliability of a mean is a direct function of the reliability of the measure being analyzed, whereas the reliability of a covariance is a joint function of the reliabilities of the two measures comprising the covariance. For example, the reliability of a simple ordinary least squares (OLS) Pearson correlation is the product of the reliabilities of the two measures being correlated. The upshot of all this for designing a diary study is that it takes more observations to model the variability in less reliable coefficients than to model the variability in more reliable coefficients. Also, similar to OLS analyses, there is also the issue of the size of a relationship itself. It is easier to "find" larger covariances than it is to find smaller ones. This applies to covariances both within levels and between levels.

Underlying all this is the frequency with which events and states of interest occur. For this discussion, I will refer to these events and states as "targets." In important ways, the frequency with which a target occurs contributes to the reliability of coefficients that describe or make an inference about the target. For example, negative social situations (e.g., overt conflict) and feeling fear are relatively uncommon in most people's lives. As discussed in the previous section (length of study), a study needs to be long enough to "capture" a reasonable number of instances of the target. How many is reasonable? Frankly, I know of no formal basis that can serve as a basis for a recommendation.

Noting this, I (again) recommend that researchers keep in mind that diary-level observations constitute samples. Diary-level observations consist of a sample of observations taken from a population of diary-level targets: interactions, days, situations, and so forth. When designing a diary study, researchers need to take into account the number of observations that are needed to constitute a sample from which inferences can be drawn. The ability of diary-level samples to provide a firm basis for inference will depend upon the target of inference. If a researcher is interested primarily in estimating population parameters of coefficients representing diary-level phenomena, then the number of targets that occur across the entire sample (across all persons) is the critical consideration. For example, if questions of interest concern differences in affect between conflictual and non-conflictual social interactions, then the strength of inference will depend upon the total number of conflictual interactions, assuming most interactions are not conflictual.

More often than not, however, questions of interest concern person-level differences in such within-person relationships, e.g., relationships between a personality trait such as agreeableness and differences in affective reactions to conflictual and non-conflictual interactions. In such instances, researchers need to consider the number of target observations collected for each person. The number of target observations affects the reliability of the coefficients representing those observations. All things being equal, more observations provide more reliable estimates. There may be instances, however, when target observations are simply not common, and the resulting coefficients may necessarily be unreliable. In such cases, researchers can compensate for the likely unreliability of such coefficients by increasing the number of persons in a study.

Targets that occur (very) infrequently may also call into question the validity of using a diary approach. There is the possibility that what was initially conceptualized as a within-person relationship may be best studied through some type of between-person design. The death of a loved one is typically an isolated event, and unless there is some reason to expect this will happen (e.g., participants have spouses in cancer treatment), modeling within-person variability with this event as a focus is likely to involve a lot of extraneous data collection. In other words, the benefits of within-person comparisons (e.g., a person serves as their own control) may be outweighed by the costs of collecting a lot of data.

Finally, if target events and states are very infrequent, this raises the possibility that researchers should treat the existence of a target occasion as a between-person measure. For example, if a study concerns the influence of the death of a spouse on reactions to daily hassles, rather than examine such influences as a within-person phenomenon, they could be examined at the between-person level. Participants who had a spouse die within a certain period could be compared to those who had not. Moreover, even when a target is frequent, the presence or absence of the target may need to be treated as a between-person variable for some purposes.

Sample size and power: Tentative recommendations

For most purposes, my experience suggests that for a study of daily processes, two weeks of daily data and 100 participants should suffice; 75 participants is not bad, below 50 it gets dicey, 150 is very nice, and much more than 150 seems to be overkill. As discussed above, I think a study of two weeks is much better than a study of one week, but I am not certain that three weeks is much better than two weeks primarily because of the possible decline in the quality of the data. When thinking of sample sizes (both within and between person), researchers need to keep in mind that the marginal cost of adding a participant is usually quite low. The bulk of the "cost" of a diary study is setting up the infrastructure – designing the instruments and recruiting the participants. A study in which there are 75 participants is rarely (if ever) 1.5 times as "expensive" as a study in which there are 50 participants. For a more nuanced discussion, see West, Ryu, Kwok, and Cham (2011).

Recently, Bolger, Stadler, and Laurenceau (2012) proposed estimating power by using simulations that include parameter estimates based upon pilot studies or previous research. Their approach is somewhat limited in that it is not a formal model. Moreover, it does not cover event contingent designs and does not include all of the four types of relationships discussed above, nor does it explicitly address issues of the reliability of coefficients. Nevertheless, the general notion that simulation studies can provide meaningful insights into the power of diary-style studies is very valuable, and given the absence of coherent guidelines for such studies in the available literature, researchers may find it useful to conduct such simulations. Furthermore, the use of pilot data to provide some type of estimates of variances is certainly better than imagining what the variances might be. Eventually, such simulations could include the estimation of various types of parameters such as cross-level effects.

3

Diary-level measures

In my experience, setting up diary studies tends to be more time consuming than setting up lab studies. For some research questions, you can program a computer and run 50 participants at a time, and changes in independent and dependent measures can be done with keystrokes. Certainly, there are lab studies that take lots of time to prepare and execute, but I think that, on average, getting a meaningful number of people to provide meaningful data on a repeated basis takes more time than getting a meaningful number of people to provide meaningful data once, or occasionally, or a few times.

Regardless of differences between lab and diary research, setting up a diary study can take a good deal of time and effort. Given this, I can tell you from personal experience that the temptation is great to ask as much as you can (or think of) every time a participant provides data – the urge is almost overpowering. You may have a sense that it took a lot of work to get these people in your sights (and they will not be there for too long), so you need to strike while the iron is hot. Moreover, working with undergraduate participants (who are typically serfs or acolytes or some combination thereof) leads one to think that people, in general, are willing, if not eager, to answer endless series of barely distinguishable questions over and over again.

As much as I appreciate this position (and as much as such motives have guided my behavior in the past), I recommend stepping back from such a position and being guided by such homilies as "Less is more" or "Small is beautiful" as trite as such expressions may be. When people provide data on a regular basis they may not recognize the importance of answering the same set of questions on day $n + 10$ with the same gusto (and consequentially the same validity) as they did on day n. The more items you have, the less energy/time/attention participants can devote to responding to each item.

The virtual explosion of diary-style research has been accompanied by a similar increase in the type and focus of diary-level measures. There are so many that a true summary of the entirety of them is not possible here. What I have done in this section is describe types or classes of diary-level measures. The typology I have used was not meant to be rigid; rather, I have clustered measures in a way that made sense to me. Someone else might think otherwise, and I would not challenge this. Nevertheless, I think the discussion below will help you design your study. Of course, your overriding concerns should be your hypotheses and how to collect the measures that will provide a basis to test these hypotheses. Bon voyage.

Temporal indicators

I use the descriptor "temporal indicator" to refer to measures representing when a diary entry was provided and the time the entry is meant to describe. Although a researcher may not place much importance on temporal aspects per se of the data in a study (e.g., the day of the week data were collected), I strongly recommend obtaining temporal indicators if possible. First, such indicators are needed to demonstrate that participants complied with the data collection protocol of the study. For example, were the data in a daily diary study *in fact* provided on a daily basis? Second, a researcher's interests may change to include a focus on temporal indicators (e.g., weekends vs. weekdays), and it is typically impossible to reconstitute or recreate such indicators. How can a researcher truly and reasonably estimate when data were provided when there are no data describing when the data were provided? Regardless, I recommend collecting the following indicators:

1 The date and time the responses were provided, and if there is a distinction, the date and time the target of the description occurred. In an interval contingent study, these two indicators will be roughly equivalent. For example, if a participant responds on Wednesday evening to a series of questions that begin with the stem "Today, I felt..." a researcher can feel reasonably confident that the responses refer to how the participant felt on Wednesday. In such cases one set of temporal indicators will suffice, and if the data are collected electronically (e.g., through a website) the collection portal can attach a date and time stamp to each entry. In an event contingent study (e.g., a social interaction diary study), it is probably best to ask explicitly when an event occurred as part of the record-level data.
2 The day of the week to which the responses refer. Most electronic portals can attach a simple 1–7 code representing the day of the week a response was entered. For pencil and paper studies, this code can be entered manually when the data are entered into a spreadsheet or data file. Also, many computer programs can create a day of the week variable from a date variable. The day of the week code may need to be modified before the data are analyzed (see section on data preparation), but such a code is relatively easy to collect or create.
3 An indicator of the temporal sequence of the data. To me, the easiest way to do this is to use what is called a "Julian date." For Julian dates (which are not dates per se, but are numbers), January 1 = 1, January 2 = 2, and so forth. The Julian date provides a simple basis to sort and organize data, and, perhaps more important, it provides a simple basis to determine how or if lagged variables should be calculated. For example, if the difference in Julian dates between observation n and observation $n + 1$ is more than 1, then a lagged variable (for lag = 1 day) cannot be calculated.

Controlling for non-random sampling at the diary level

Unlike the controlled stimuli and situations in laboratory studies, by definition and design, the events and situations that individuals experience in their daily lives will differ. Depending upon the hypotheses of interest, you may need to take such differences into account. For example, assume that you are interested in relationships between agreeableness and how people resolve arguments, and you have conducted an event contingent study in which the target event is an argument. It may be that some people argue only with personal friends and not with co-workers, whereas other people argue with only co-workers and not with friends. If this is true, analyses that do not take such a difference into account run the risk of being confounded. To continue the example, suppose that people who argue with only friends are low in agreeableness, whereas people who argue with only co-workers are high in agreeableness. Analyses that examined relationships between agreeableness and how arguments are resolved should take into account the differences in the types of arguments people had. It might be that arguments with co-workers are in and of themselves more easily resolved than arguments with friends. If so, relationships between agreeableness and ease of resolving arguments would be confounded by the relationship between agreeableness and the type of argument people experience. Such a confound would not invalidate the relationship between agreeableness and resolving arguments. The relationship between agreeableness and resolving arguments would still exist. Such a confound would simply provide another level of explanation.

The same type of natural and unavoidable confound can also occur in interval and signal contingent studies. For example, in a study of relationships between stress and self-esteem, the types of stressors that individuals experience may vary as a function of self-esteem. If this is true, then individual differences in within-person relationships between stress and self-esteem may reflect differences in the types of stressors that people experience. As in the previous example, such a confound would not invalidate the relationship between stress and self-esteem, but it would provide another level of explanation.

There is no formula, no quick and simple solution, for this. You cannot change people's daily lives and eliminate the differences in them; this would undermine the validity of the diary study itself. Nevertheless, you need to anticipate the possibility that the life situations people experience will vary, perhaps in ways that weaken the strength of the inferences you draw. The best way to deal with such possibilities is to collect the type of data that will allow you to control statistically the differences in people's lives that you cannot manipulate directly. Exactly how this is accomplished will vary as a function of the participant sample and the focus of your study. Some hints about the need for such controls and how they can be accomplished can probably be had by some type of pretesting. Often, a few simple questions can address such issues, but the questions must be included in the protocol if the analyses are to control for the differences they represent.

Self-reports: Scales and questionnaires

Self-report measures are probably the most common type of measure used by personality and social psychologists. Although many psychologists find self-reports lacking, there are constructs such as internal emotional states or feelings of satisfaction for which self-reports are well suited. Not all appreciate this position, however. For example, a reviewer of a version of a manuscript describing a RIR-based study (at a journal other than that in which the study was published) was critical of the fact that we measured enjoyment of social interaction with a self-report measure (Nezlek & Pilkington, 1994). As is standard practice, we simply asked participants how enjoyable their interactions were. The reviewer was concerned that participants would/did not know how enjoyable their interactions were.

We were flummoxed by this comment. Admittedly, there are internal states and processes of which people are not aware, but we did not think that a straightforward rating of how pleasurable social interactions were relied upon inaccessible states or processes. Moreover, if the validity of such self-reports is denied, then most diary studies have little validity. Most important, we had no idea how we could have measured this construct using some type of "objective" measure – nor for that matter was one suggested. We did think about having participants put their fingers into some type of physiological data collection port when they were responding, but we passed on that. The data were already collected, and we would have had to rewire the campus. The bottom line is that diary researchers are probably going to be using self-report measures of various types for the foreseeable future. Certainly they have their limitations, but this does not mean they should be relegated to the trash heap. See Stone, Turkkan, Bachrach, Jobe, Kurtzman, and Cain (2000), an edited volume about self-reports, for a through treatment of this issue.

One of the tensions in designing self-report measures is that between thoroughness/completeness of coverage and efficiency/economy. Unfortunately, there seems to be a norm among some researchers that "more is more" when it comes to scale construction. The field is awash with scales that measure a single construct with 20 (or more) items. Such a tendency may be spurred on by the fact that Cronbach's alpha, the most common measure of reliability, increases as the number of items in a scale increases, assuming the same average inter-item correlation. Nevertheless, my reading of the psychometrics literature is that there is an increasing interest or emphasis on shorter scales with fewer, better items. For example, and consistent with such an emphasis, Robins, Hendin, and Trzesniewski (2001) suggested that self-esteem can be reliably and validly measured with a single item.

Aside from questions about the number of items that are needed to measure a construct accurately, researchers need to keep in mind that participants in diary studies typically provide diary-level measures on a frequent and regular basis (recall the sometimes used label "intensive repeated measures design"). Although the Rosenberg Self-Esteem Scale (Rosenberg, 1965) has 10 items, and it may be that using 10 items is better than using less than 10 items (putting aside Robins et al. for the moment), I do not think it is practical (or appropriate) to ask participants to answer 10 (sort of) redundant questions over and over again. They will get bored and become inattentive.

In fact, non-student participants may find it tedious to answer what seems to be a small number of questions on trait measures (small for researchers used to compliant students). For example, in pilot testing for the study described in Schaafsma, Nezlek, Krejtz, and Safron (2010) community members (not students) found it tedious (and some balked) at completing trait measures that had 12 items. For the final study, we administered versions with six items.

Moreover, given the high internal consistency (e.g., high inter-item correlations at the trait level) of many scales, particularly the self-esteem scale, it does not seem that 10 items are needed to provide a reasonable measure of self-esteem. In my own research I have used four self-esteem items taken from the trait measure (see Nezlek, 2005). Later, I provide some recommendations for constructing diary-level measures of constructs that may be traditionally thought of as traits.

Authors will need to be wary of the fact that some reviewers will not appreciate the need to use fewer (and perhaps somewhat different) items to measure constructs at the diary level than is used at the trait level. For example, a reviewer of Nezlek et al. (2008b), at a journal other than that in which the study was published, took us to task for using only 4 items of the 10 items from the Rosenberg Self-Esteem Scale to measure daily self-esteem. The reviewer insisted that measuring self-esteem as Rosenberg conceptualized it required using all 10 items on the trait measure. Anything else was simply not, and could not be, a valid measure of self-esteem.

The fundamental flaw in this critique is the assumption that scores on a scale (per se) are the construct – an individual's score on the Rosenberg *is* that person's self-esteem. Responses to these particular items, and these items alone, are self-esteem. In contrast, measurement theory (as widely accepted within the social sciences) posits that scores are observed (or manifest) measures of latent (or underlying) constructs. A person's score on the Rosenberg is simply *a measure* of that person's self-esteem, and if fewer items produce scores that are functionally equivalent to scores produced with more items, so what?

In addition to being conservative in terms of the number of items that are used to measure each construct, researchers need to be conservative in terms of the number of constructs that are being measured. Once again, keep in mind that participants have a fixed amount of cognitive resources. The more responses they asked to provide, the less attention they can give to any particular response. When requesting measures of multiple constructs, researchers need to be certain that participants understand and appreciate the differences among the constructs being measured. Differences that may be obvious to academic researchers may be unclear (or even non-existent) to lay people. Typically, I try to do this by providing detailed instructions that discuss what items concern and what they do not concern. See the appendix "Social interaction diary instructions" for sample instructions.

A good example of the influence that increasing the number of responses can have on how well participants distinguish constructs can be had from my own research. In the first RIR study (Wheeler & Nezlek, 1977) and the second (my dissertation, Nezlek, 1993 – I know, it took a while for me to publish the data) participants provided two ratings of each interaction, satisfaction and intimacy. Each used a 1–7 scale, and intimacy was reverse scored (1 = very intimate). In contrast, in most studies that followed (my own and others'), participants provided more ratings of each interaction (e.g., nine ratings in Leary, Nezlek, Downs, Radford-Davenport, Martin, and McMullen (1994)). In these later studies, within-person relationships between intimacy and enjoyment are meaningfully stronger than they are in the early studies. In the early studies, the two ratings were functionally unrelated.

I should add that relationships in the later studies were not so strong as to suggest that the two measures did not possess discriminant validity. Nevertheless, when making nine ratings, participants did not distinguish satisfaction and intimacy as much as when they were making only two ratings. I shudder to think of the possible lack of discriminant validity of individual ratings in studies in which 10, 20, or more responses are provided multiple times each day. Even if participants are highly motivated, I suspect that as the number of items increases, responses to specific items are influenced more by the hedonic dimension described by Osgood, Suci, and Tannenbaum (1957). This would be reflected in higher correlations between items as more of the variance in each item reflects a simple global good–bad rating.

Another way to increase the accuracy of diary-level measures (and measures in general) is to maximize the correspondence between the construct being measured and the scale labels being used to measure it. In most instances, researchers are interested in how much, how well, or how strongly an individual thinks or feels in terms of some specific dimension. For example, "How enjoyable was the interaction?" Such a measure reflects the strength or magnitude of some underlying construct, and the accompanying rating scale should consist of some type of "magnitude estimation" scale. For example, a 1–7 scale in which 1 represents not at all and 7 represents very much, strongly, and so forth.

I recommend avoiding the over- (and inappropriately) used Likert-style scale with which respondents indicate their relative agreement or disagreement with a target statement. For example, as a measure of how enjoyable an interaction was, respondents could be asked to indicate how much they agree with a statement such as "I enjoyed the interaction." Although measures obtained using such response scales are probably not grossly inadequate or inaccurate, they insert a level of interpretation between the response scale and the construct being measured. At a pure linguistic level, an individual who enjoyed an interaction immensely could respond "disagree" to a statement indicating that he or she simply enjoyed it. I realize such a possibility is a bit forced, but if we think of items on questionnaires as questions we would ask people, to find out how someone felt about an interaction most people would probably not solicit someone's agreement with a statement such as "I enjoyed the interaction." In common discourse, we would be more likely to ask someone how much he or she enjoyed an interaction, and the person would reply with some type of magnitude estimate – a lot, a little, not at all, and so forth.

Regardless of the exact scale being used, researchers need to do their utmost to ensure that scale intervals are as close to equal as possible. I think the notion of "equally appearing" intervals is given a bit of lip service – everyone acknowledges that it is important, but not everyone takes the task seriously. The classic reference (in my mind) is Cliff (1959). Cliff presents empirically based recommendations for adverbs that will create scales with equal intervals. Although it may not be the be-all and end-all, it is a good place to start.

My goal in discussing these issues is to help you ensure that your measures are "light and tight." Participants will be answering the questions you ask them over and over, and it is in your best interests to minimize their fatigue and boredom by making it easy to answer the questions you pose. You might be thinking, "Well, if I am asking a question on a repeated basis, won't the error associated with fatigue, boredom, and differing interpretations balance out?" If analyses were concerned with only within-person means, you might have a point (to an extent). One of my concerns in addressing this issue is the fact that many hypotheses will concern relationships (covariances) between measures, and unreliability wreaks meaningfully more havoc with estimates of covariances than it does with estimates of means, particularly when the number of observations is low.

Diary-level measures of traits

A common distinction within personality theory is that between states and traits. Although specific definitions vary, psychological traits such as the characteristics that are known as the Big Five (FFM) are assumed to be relatively consistent across time, whereas states are assumed to vary across time. Nevertheless, it is possible to conceptualize the same construct as both a state and a trait. Within the present context, some diary-level measures can be considered as state-level measures of traits.

One of the better known measures that distinguishes states and traits is probably Spielberger's classic State–Trait Anxiety Inventory (STAI; Spielberger, Gorsuch, & Lushene, 1970). To measure trait anxiety, respondents indicate how they "generally feel" using a 1–4 scale with response options labeled almost never, sometimes, often, and almost always. The 20 target statements include items such as "I feel nervous and restless" and "I am a steady person." To measure state anxiety, respondents also answer 20 questions, with the stem "indicate how you feel right now, that is, at this very moment." The response scale has four options, with labels of not at all, a little, somewhat, and very much so. The state items are not exactly the same as the trait items, although some are quite similar (e.g., "I feel nervous," and "I feel steady.").

Although the state scale of the STAI is well validated, as are other state-level measures of constructs that are typically considered as traits (e.g., self-esteem, Heatherton & Polivy, 1991), many such measures are not appropriate for use as diary-level measures. Put simply, they have too many items. For example, both the state anxiety and self-esteem scales just mentioned have 20 items. As discussed above, the "return on investment" of measuring a single construct with 20 items on a repeated basis is simply not worth it.

Here is a strategy that I have found useful to create state-level analogs of constructs traditionally conceptualized as traits. The underlying rationale is to create state-level measures based upon trait-level measures of the corresponding construct. The process is simple. Examine the items used to measure the construct at the trait level and then select a small set of these items (2–4) and modify them to administer at the state level. Selection can be based on factor loadings and on appropriateness for repeated administration, with some rewording.

For example, in a series of studies I have measured self-esteem using four items based on the trait version of the Rosenberg Self-Esteem Scale. The Rosenberg scale has positive and negative valenced items, and the four daily items I have used include two of each. Each item was reworded slightly from the original. For example, the original trait item "All in all, I am inclined to feel like a failure" was reworded to "Today, I felt like a failure." Even more directly, the original trait item "On the whole, I am satisfied with myself" was reworded to "Today, on the whole, I was satisfied with myself." These items are in an appendix. The ease with which this can be done will vary across measures, but in most cases it should be quite feasible.

How to estimate the reliability of a set of items as a measure of a single construct is discussed later in a separate section. One way to estimate the validity of such a measure is to examine the relationship between diary-level means and a person-level (dispositional) measure of the same construct. This assumes that the typical (mean) state level of a measure should correspond to a trait-level measure of the same construct. This validity can be expressed in terms of the variance shared between a trait and a mean state, a topic discussed in the sections on effect sizes and on evaluating reliability and validity. An example of estimating the validity of a state-level measure using this procedure can be found in Nezlek and Plesko (2001).

In the appendix "Diary-level measures," I have provided a list of diary-level measures that were created by rewording trait-level measures. The list is not meant to be a complete list of all that is possible or that has been done (far from it). Rather, it is simply illustrative of what is possible.

Measures of events

In interval contingent studies, it is common to collect some type of measure of external circumstances. Often, this will consist of some type of checklist: which of the following occurred or was occurring, and so forth? Although researchers need to collect the data that they need, to test the hypotheses that are the focus of their studies, I offer the following suggestions. First, and perhaps most important, such measures should reflect some type of framework or model about the aspects of the environment that are germane to the processes of interest. My sense is that most researchers have a reasonable idea about this, but describing this basis explicitly can help readers understand why certain events/circumstances were measured and others were not.

In the appendix "Diary-level measures," I have provided an example of an event schedule based upon a relatively simple framework. The schedule was designed to measure daily events in terms of two dimensions, positive vs. negative, crossed with social vs. achievement domains. The positive–negative distinction reflects the well-documented difference between positive and negative stimuli across a wide variety of domains (e.g., Baumeister, Bratslavsky, Finkenauer, & Vohs, 2001). The distinction between the social and achievement domains reflects a longstanding distinction in psychology between work and love, agency and communion, and so forth, hearkening to Freud's "Arbeit und Lieben."

Regardless of the specific framework, I think it is best to measure both positive and negative events/circumstances (e.g., hassles and uplifts, à la Kanner, Coyne, Schaefer, & Lazarus, 1981). Much of the daily diary work done through the 1990s concerned only negative daily events (see Nezlek & Plesko, 2003, for a brief discussion). Although valuable, a full understanding of how people react to external circumstances requires attention to positive circumstances. For example, Nezlek and Plesko (2003) and Nezlek and Allen (2006) found that daily positive events buffered the impact of daily negative events. Negative events had less of an impact on well-being on days when there were more positive events than on days when there were fewer positive events. Moreover, positive events themselves are important to consider. In a series of daily diary studies, I have found that positive events are related to a variety of outcomes above and beyond the influence of negative events (e.g., Nezlek, 2005). For a more detailed discussion of the importance of considering the positive aspects of daily life see Gable and Reis (2010).

There is also the issue of response scales. Although I certainly appreciate the need for simplicity when designing diary-level measures, measuring something more than "did X happen?" does not need to take a lot more energy than the simple yes/no. Moreover, some type of rating of events provides the basis for computing composite scores. There are two basic ways to score measures of events, frequency counts and composite scores. As suggested by the title, frequency counts are simply tallies of the number of events that have occurred. Events are not differentiated or distinguished. In contrast, composite scores are weighted averages. If events are rated in terms of meaningfulness, importance, and so forth, events that are more important are given more weight.

I prefer composite scores over frequency counts. Psychometrically, composite scores are more stable. Within-person variances of composite scores are more similar across people than the variances of frequency counts, the variances for scores representing different types of events are more similar, and distributions are more normal. Moreover, composite scores are the standard in the life events literature (e.g., Sarason, Johnson, & Siegel, 1978), which in some ways is the forerunner of the daily events literature.

Regardless of the types of events or circumstances that are measured and how they are measured, I strongly recommend researchers not to limit measures to "the single most important event," or "the single most meaningful situational variable," or something to that effect. Such selectivity runs contrary to the raison d'être of diary research. Moreover, it probably introduces all sorts of biases in terms of recall and selection. The guiding principle of diary-style research is to measure what happened in ways that reduce recall biases. Certainly, participants can indicate which event or situation they thought was the most meaningful of the day (or time period), but they should do this as part of a full description.

In the appendix "Diary-level measures," I have presented an event schedule that I have used in a few daily event studies. Know that I have not provided this schedule assuming that it represents the be-all and end-all for measuring daily events or events occurring within any other timeframe. Quite the opposite, I have provided this schedule simply as an example of how events can be measured. As discussed in this appendix, participants are asked to rate each event, providing a basis for computing frequency and composite scores.

Circumplex or grid-based measures

The preceding discussion has concerned measuring unidimensional constructs, i.e., constructs that can be measured using scales that vary in terms of only one dimension at a time. Nevertheless, there are some constructs that have been discussed in terms of multidimensional spaces, and for diary studies I think two of these constructs are particularly relevant. One is commonly referred to as the affect grid and the other is the interpersonal circumplex. In both cases, a single assessment represents an individual's position in a two-dimensional space, and consequently a single assessment provides two measures, one on each dimension of the two-dimensional space. To provide responses within a circumplex or grid system, individuals select a specific point on a grid.

I will illustrate this type of response using the affect grid (Russell, Weiss, & Mendelsohn, 1989), which is presented below. The quadrant in which the response is selected represents the combination of valence and arousal of the affect an individual is experiencing or describing. For example, positive active emotions (e.g., happy) are located in the upper right-hand quadrant, whereas negative active emotions (e.g., anxiousness) are in the lower right-hand quadrant. The distance from the origin (the center of the grid) represents the strength or intensity of the feeling. For example, a response in the lower left-hand quadrant that was near the origin would indicate mild negative deactive feelings (e.g., being a little sad), whereas a response in the lower left-hand quadrant that was far from the origin would indicate strong feelings of sadness.

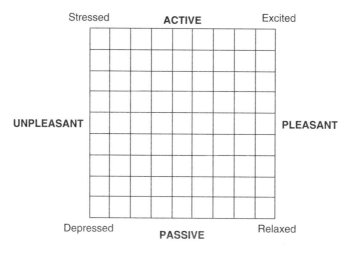

Figure 3.1   Affect grid (Reproduced with permission of Peter Kuppens, Department of Psychology, University of Leuven, Belgium.)

The other circumplex model that is well suited for diary studies (particularly social interaction diary research) is an interpersonal circumplex based upon a typology employed by Moskowitz (1994). The interpersonal circumplex is structurally identical to the affect grid except that the two axes represent two dimensions of interpersonal behavior: agreeable–quarrelsome and dominant–submissive. In turn, the quadrants formed by combining these two dimensions are agreeable+dominant, agreeable+submissive, quarrelsome+submissive, and quarrelsome+dominant. I have used this circumplex in a social interaction diary study. Participants described their behavior during the interaction by selecting a point on the grid. These data have not been analyzed yet, but participants reported few problems using the grid.

Such circumplex measures provide both advantages and disadvantages over single dimension assessments. One important advantage is the fact that one response can be used to generate scores on two dimensions simultaneously. Exactly how these two scores would be generated would depend upon the specific way in which the grid was displayed and the data coded at entry. Correspondingly, it would take at least two single dimension items to generate a point in a two-dimensional space. Another advantage of collecting data within the framework of a circumplex is that it provides a basis to calculate measures of within-person variability within a circumplex, as described in the section on analyses of instability. One possibly important disadvantage of a circumplex measure is a lack of specificity compared to single-item measures. For example, it is difficult, if not impossible, to generate measures of specific emotions from an affective circumplex measure.

Automatically generated measures

My guess is that when most personality and social psychologists think of a diary study, they think of collecting some type of self-report measures as I have just discussed. Participants consciously and actively provide some type of response to describe how they thought or felt or what happened at some type of interval or as the result of some type of an event. There are, however, other options, which I believe will increase in number over time.

Many of these options fall into a broad category that is frequently referred to as "ambulatory assessment" – assessing people while they are ambulatory. As an aside, much of research that is described as "AA" has its origins in health psychology or medicine, and although many US researchers use ambulatory assessment methods, my sense is that their use is a bit more common in Europe. The number and variety of measures that can be obtained using such methods are increasing on a constant basis. They presently include, but are not limited to, heart rate, blood pressure, respiration, bodily movement, and, apparently, even hormone levels. Although the devices vary in terms of how intrusive they are (size, interference with movement, etc.), over time they have become less intrusive, and I suspect that this trend will continue.

The complexity and specifics of these different technologies make it difficult to describe or discuss them in meaningful detail in this volume. Moreover, my sense is that, at present, they are not used widely by social and personality psychologists per se. Nevertheless, I expect that as social and personality psychologists include more physiologically based measures in their research, the use of such automatically generated measures will become more commonplace. Some of these methods are described in various chapters in Mehl and Conner (2012). For a discussion of the use of psychophysiological measures in more lab-based settings, see Blascovich, Vanman, Mendes, and Dickerson (2011), another volume in this series.

One technique that generates data automatically and that is used by personality and social psychologists is what has come to be called the EAR (Electronically Activated Recorder; Mehl, Pennebaker, Crow, Dabbs, & Price, 2001). In short, people wear the EAR and it records sounds (in the immediate environment) at predetermined intervals (e.g., 50-second intervals every 9 minutes). Participants need to do nothing to initiate these recordings. Participants report that they become accustomed to the EAR quickly and that they do not find it intrusive. Recent research suggests that a two-day sample provides reliable estimates of various categories that have been studied to date. For more detailed information about the EAR go to http://dingo.sbs.arizona.edu/~mehl/EAR.htm (as July 2011) and see Mehl (2007).

To me, the great challenge of using the EAR is analyzing the data. Keep in mind that the data are raw sounds – literally, whatever sounds were in the range of the device when it was switched on. This includes voices as well as sounds from the non-social environment (cars, radios, anything). Researchers need to design protocols to guide coding of samples, and then the samples need to be coded to measure the constructs of interest. Moreover, a study using the EAR can provide a lot of information. If the EAR is switched on for 50 seconds every 9 minutes, this will produce 960 segments of 50 seconds for a 16-hour day. Even if many of those segments are totally quiet, for a two-day study there will still be a considerable number of segments that need to be coded for each participant.

When people are talking, the EAR collects speech samples, and the analysis of speech is a discipline in itself. Although there are various options to analyze speech, researchers may want to consider the Linguistic Inquiry and Word Count program (LIWC; Pennebaker, Booth, & Francis, 2007). The LIWC takes raw text files and provides a variety of summary measures. Moreover, it is customizable. Words and categories can be added to the base package to provide counts of specific constructs in which an investigator might be interested.

Ways of collecting data

Given how rapidly communication technologies are evolving, I am reluctant to spend too much time describing how to use specific technologies to conduct diary studies. What is *au courant* as I write this draft of this volume may be *passé* by the time the volume is published. Nevertheless, there are some issues that merit consideration.

Initially, and before the dramatic innovations in technology and communication we as a society are now experiencing, most diary research was conducted using what is commonly referred to as "pencil and paper" methods. Participants were given blank forms and were told to complete them on a certain basis. Completed forms might be collected at the end of a study or at intervals during the study. Collecting at intervals during a study allowed (and allows) researchers to monitor participants' compliance with the data collection protocol more closely.

Pencil and paper methods have numerous advantages compared to collecting diary data mechanically/electronically. They are relatively inexpensive. They require no specialized knowledge or skills on the part of the researchers. No one needs to know the latest and greatest interface, website development platform, or micro-programming language. Researchers can design forms, duplicate them, and distribute them to participants. Moreover, the more direct personal contact there is between researchers and participants, the better. There is no substitute for personal contact.

Similarly, for participants, when using pencil and paper measures they simply need to know how to read (and perhaps write). They do not need to own (or be given) any sort of electronic device, nor do they need to know how to operate one. They do not need to have constant and reliable access to the Internet or to some type of communications network. There are no downtimes. Failing networks, poor connections, computer viruses, and so forth are irrelevant (sounds attractive to me). You just need to be certain that participants have (or have access to) enough forms – they can always borrow a pencil or pen.

Now, for the drawbacks. First and perhaps most important, electronic data collection can provide a much better basis for evaluating participant compliance than that provided by pencil and paper methods. I know of no electronic portal that cannot provide date and time stamps for entries. Entries that are not provided within an appropriate window can be deleted. I discuss deleting data in the next chapter. Second, it is much (much) easier to manage the data provided by electronic portals. Although the data produced by some devices may seem unwieldy, invariably, preparing data for analysis that have been collected using some type of electronic method is much easier than preparing data that have been collected using pencil and paper. Most pencil and paper data need to be entered by hand into some type of data management system (SPSS, Excel, and the like). Given the number of measures and the differences among them (numbers and perhaps letters), data entry mistakes are inevitable. They simply cannot be totally avoided. In contrast, data that are entered electronically typically conform to the requirements for analysis. Numbers are where they should be, letters are where they should be, and so forth.

There exists a vigorous debate about the relative merits of using paper and pencil methods to collect diary data versus using more automated, electronically based methods. In fact, this debate was the focus of five articles published in an issue of *Psychological Methods* (2006, vol. 11, pp. 87–125). The upshot of this debate seems to be that paper and pencil diaries provide data that are sufficiently valuable so that researchers should feel confident using them. They have their shortcomings, but they are not fatally or fundamentally flawed.

Regardless of the relative merits or shortcomings of paper and pencil methods compared to electronic methods, there may be times when paper and pencil methods need to be used. For example, in Schaafsma et al. (2010) we used a social interaction diary to study the social interactions of Muslim immigrants in the Netherlands and Poland. Our participants did not have access to the Internet or telecommunications networks, and most were unfamiliar with social science research methods. Using simple written forms helped to reduce the strangeness of what they were doing.

Even when participants are familiar with social science research methods and have access to electronic networks, such access may not be sufficiently regular to allow for uninterrupted data collection. For example, some participants in a social interaction diary study conducted in Germany (Nezlek, Schütz, & Sellin, 2007) and a daily diary study with some participants in Japan (Nezlek et al., 2008b) did not have Internet access all the time during the study. They were given paper forms to complete for the days for which they did not have access.

Regardless of how the data are collected, researchers need to provide evidence (at least some evidence) that participants complied with the data collection protocol. The more objective the evidence (e.g., electronic date and time stamps), the better. Nevertheless, even if it is not possible to collect objective indices, it is possible to collect some indication of participant compliance. For example, in the early work using the RIR, electronic data collection was simply not an option. Participants described their interactions using a standardized paper form, with 3–4 interactions per page. At the end of the study, participants were interviewed individually, and the interviewer had the participant's data in hand. These data were examined for simple characteristics such as did the script vary from record to record? For most participants, there would be some variability in the physical records from day to day. One day might be in blue ink, another in black, a third in pencil, and so forth. What was particularly suspicious was when the impression of writing on one form was clearly on the next form, and this was the case for all the records.

Research assistants gave each participant a semi-structured interview. In this interview we requested explanations for missing days, probed about possible inaccuracies, and so forth, while assuring participants that they would be paid (or credit awarded). Participants were asked to describe the ways in which they did not follow the protocol, with the understanding that we (the researchers) would prefer to drop them from the analyses (with no hard feelings) rather than draw conclusions based upon inaccurate data. As discussed in the previous section on participant commitment, soliciting such information depends very much on the quality of the relationship between participants and researchers.

Between-person measures

I have discussed diary-level measures in detail because I suspect that many readers are relatively unfamiliar with them, and, after all, this is a book about diary methods. Nevertheless, diary studies are best conceptualized as nested designs in which repeated (diary-level) measures are collected for a sample of persons, and it is possible (and typically desirable) to collect measures that describe people per se. Such measures can include demographic characteristics such as sex and ethnicity, personality characteristics such as the traits of the Five-Factor Model, measures of social identity, and so forth. The essential defining difference between diary-level measures and person-level measures is that person-level measures do not vary over the course of a study. They are constant. Demographic characteristics such as sex do not change, and for most intents and purposes, characteristics such as personality, social identity, and so forth, do not change, or it is presumed they do not change.

Any measure that does change over the course of a study is by definition a diary-level measure, irrespective of what it was intended to be. For example, if a trait measure of the Five-Factor Model is collected every day, even though the measure is technically and conceptually intended to be a measure of a construct that does not change day to day, if there is day-level variance in the measure, then it must be treated as a day-level (diary) measure. On the other hand, any measure that does not change over the course of a study is by definition a person-level measure, irrespective of what it was intended to be. For example, if a measure of trust in others is collected for every social interaction, even though the measure is intended to be a measure of a construct that changes across interactions, if there is no interaction-level variance in the measure, then it must be treated as a person-level measure.

It is also possible to calculate person-level summary measures of diary-level data and treat them as person-level variables. For example, if self-esteem were measured every day, the mean self-esteem for a person could be calculated and treated as a person-level variable. Such simple aggregates have some limitations that may limit their usefulness. For example, means for different people may be based on different numbers of observations, and means based on more observations may be more representative than means based on fewer observations. In addition, such aggregates may not represent a set of observations well. For example, 5 is the mean of 1, 1, 1, 9, 9, and 9, but it clearly does not represent the six observations very well. Regardless, such measures can be calculated and used.

When thinking of person-level measures within the context of diary studies there are a few issues to consider that may not be salient for studies that do not contain a diary component. As I explain later, in diary-style research, person-level measures are typically conceptualized as predictors of diary-level measures. Moreover, such an assumption is consistent with the logic of multilevel modeling. Constructs at upper levels of analysis (i.e., the person) are typically thought to be causes of outcomes at lower levels of analysis (the diary level). Such an assumption also follows the longstanding tradition in personality research that traits are relatively consistent across time and space and are thought of more as causes than as results of people's behaviors, albeit in combination with situational characteristics.

Putting aside the debate about such causal relationships, most diary studies have hypotheses or questions of interest that concern person-level phenomena of some kind. I recommend thinking of such hypotheses/questions in one of two ways:

1 Relationships between person-level measures and means of diary-level measures. For example, within the context of a social interaction diary study, what is the relationship between a person's attachment style and the intimacy they experience in

social interaction? Or, within the context of a daily diary study, what is the relationship between a trait such as openness to experience and how creative people are each day?

2 Relationships between person-level measures and within-person relationships of measures at the diary level. For example, within the context of a social interaction diary study, what is the relationship between depression and differences in the enjoyment people experience when interacting with close friends vs. strangers? Or, within the context of a daily diary study, what is the relationship between a trait such as anxiety and how strongly people react to stressful events each day?

I provide this structural typology to encourage you to think about the types of relationships between the person- and diary-level constructs you will be examining as you decide what person-level measures you will administer in your studies. Are the questions of interest more process focused (i.e., the second type mentioned above), or will they concern diary-level manifestations of person-level differences (i.e., the first type mentioned above)? Both types of relationships are equally important, but the person-level constructs that are related to means of diary-level measures may be different from those that are related to within-person relationships between diary-level measures. In addition to testing hypotheses, as discussed previously, person-level measures can also be used to examine the validity of diary-level measures. This may be particularly important when using a diary-level measure for the first time, which means that the validity of the measure has not been established.

Practically speaking, I can offer the following advice. In some diary studies I have conducted, I have administered some (perhaps half) of the person-level measures before the diary component of the study begins, and then administered the rest after the diary component is done. I do this because I believe that dividing the measures reduces the likelihood that participants become bored by answering a host of questions at the same time. For example, many measures of dispositional characteristics have 20 or more items. When deciding which measures to include in the first and second halves, to minimize sensitizing participants, I tend to put measures that may be more reactive in the second half. Although I have not had many problems with such issues, if you are measuring a construct that might cause people to be more sensitive to certain issues (e.g., attitudes about out-group members), asking after they have provided the diary data may be best.

Given the present emphasis in the discipline, I think it is wise to err on the liberal side in terms of the number of dispositional measures you administer. In this case, more is more. There is considerable interest in person-level moderators of within-person (diary-level) relationships, and the more dispositional measures you collect, the more you will able to contribute to the literature on this topic. Moreover, and no different from single level studies, collecting measures of related constructs allows one to determine more specifically the unique relationships that individual measures have with an outcome.

4

Data preparation

Although electronic data collection methods have helped "clean up" the data produced by diary studies in comparison to data collected via pencil and paper, diary data are inherently more messy than the data collected in most surveys and experiments. Overall, researchers need to be prepared to spend more time preparing data from diary studies than they might spend preparing data from more traditional lab or survey studies, and in this chapter, I discuss some of the issues that arise when preparing diary data for analysis and how to deal with them.

This discussion assumes that there are two data sets: one consisting of the within-person (diary) records and another consisting of the between-person data (e.g., trait-level data). Although these two data sets may be merged for analysis (depending upon the analyses and software involved) they should be treated separately in terms of data preparation. I will not discuss how to prepare trait-level data for analysis. Readers of this volume should be familiar with such procedures.

As a guiding principle, data should be prepared in a way that provides the maximum flexibility for future analyses. Any type of code that might be used should be created. Admittedly, as analyses progress, an analyst may realize that some type of code is needed that was not anticipated at the outset, but it is much easier to create a bunch of codes at once than it is to go back to the raw data. For example, in a daily diary study, I might code days for whether they were weekend days or weekdays, using both dummy codes and a contrast code. The advantages and uses of each coding scheme are discussed later in the section on categorical predictors. I might do the same for days at work vs. days not at work. In a social interaction diary study, I might use dummy and contrast codes representing whether a close friend was present in an interaction. Note that there is a learning curve to all this. As you become more familiar with your study and its subtleties, you will have a better understanding of the possible ways in which the data can be analyzed, and this will change how the data are prepared.

Most important, all irregularities in the data need to be resolved at the outset. Invariably, an irregularity that is not relevant for one set of analyses is relevant for another set of analyses. For example, for a first set of analyses, the specific day on which an interaction occurred is not important, and so if this datum is not coded accurately, there are no consequences. Just as night follows day, however, another set of analyses will need this datum, and the irregularities will be important. And invariably, it takes more time to correct such irregularities after the data have been prepared and analyzed to test the first set of hypotheses than it takes to resolve all the irregularities at the outset. Finally, once the data are cleaned and all irregularities are resolved, analysts can proceed without "looking back over their shoulders" worrying about whether certain irregularities were not handled properly. This can include not only further analyses of the data set at hand, but also analyses in which the current data set is combined with other data. I discuss below some common issues and present recommendations for resolving them.

Moreover, I *strongly* recommend that researchers retain written documentation of what they did. A written record of what was done (e.g., diary entries and participants that were deleted) is needed to address concerns expressed by reviewers about the quality of the data on which an article is based. If authors describe a study as a "daily diary study," it behooves them to document the fact that participants provided data on a daily basis. No study is perfect, and perfection is not a reasonable standard. Nevertheless, reviewers and readers have the right to know the circumstances under which the data were collected.

Representing when data were provided and the period they are meant to describe

It is essential for analysts to know when the data they are analyzing were collected and the period of time the responses are meant to describe. First, and perhaps most important, this is needed to determine how well participants complied with the data collection protocol. For example, if data were supposed to be provided once a day at the end of the day, was this done? Some data from some participants or all the data from some participants might need to be excluded from the analyses if data were not provided in compliance with protocol. This issue is discussed below. Second, certain types of analyses may require identifying when data were collected. For example, an analyst interested in comparing weekends to weekdays needs to know the day a set of responses is meant to describe. Or, if an analyst wants to nest observations within days, the data need to be organized to allow this.

For pencil and paper studies, this is typically not much of an issue. Participants can record the date when an event such as a social interaction occurred or they can record observations that are meant to refer to a specific period of time (e.g., a day). They can also indicate when they provided these responses. Although it may not be possible to verify that the data were recorded when the participant said they were recorded, the time period to which the data refer is typically easily determined.

For data collected using some type of electronic medium (e.g., a website), representing when data were collected is simultaneously easier and more difficult. It is easier because virtually all electronic portals have the ability to record (with more precision than is typically required) when data were provided. Such descriptions can include date, time of day, day of week, and other temporal codes.

The (possible) difficulty such data present is that the "electronic" time on the record may not correspond to the "psychological time" – the life of the participant. If an individual provides responses after midnight to describe events and states that existed before midnight, then the date indicator (and all associated indicators) are moved ahead one day. The solution to this is conceptually simple.

Temporal codes need to be created that represent the psychological time. I do this by copying the temporal codes provided by the electronic portal into a new set of codes with similar names. For example, if the day of the week a record was generated is named DAYWEEK (1 = Sunday, 2 = Monday, etc.), I copy these values into a new variable NDAYWEEK. I then change NDAYWEEK as needed. For example, for a record generated at 12:15am on (technically) Thursday morning, the value of DAYWEEK (4) would be recoded to NDAYWEEK = 3 to represent the fact that the data referred to the psychological day of Wednesday. Note that Sunday = 1, and so records generated early Sunday morning are recoded to 7.

The same type of procedure needs to be applied to Julian dates (which I strongly recommend collecting). Assume a variable named JDATE is collected representing the day of the year a record was generated (January 1 = 1, January 2 = 2, etc.). Copy these data into a new variable, NJDATE, and then change NJDATE in a fashion similar to the changes made to NDAYWEEK. If a record was generated on January 5 (JDATE = 5), but the data described January 4 (JDATE = 4), then NJDATE for that record would be changed to 4.

I realize that the procedures I have just described may seem onerous. They require someone to look at individual diary entries one by one and make changes as needed. Nevertheless, even with relatively large data sets (e.g., 150 participants keeping a daily diary for two weeks), the type of inspection I describe above should not take more than a few hours, perhaps a full day at most. Of course, compliance may vary, but in my experience most participants have provided most of their data in ways that did not require any change or modification. Noting this, if a researcher has collected a very large data set with tens of thousands of observations, some type of automated procedure may be more efficient. I must conclude, however, with the observation that there is no substitute for examining the data by hand, record by record. Programs are algorithms without any flexibility or judgment, and sometimes judgment is required.

Deleting diary records and participants

One of the benefits of the type of close data inspection described above is the opportunity it provides for deleting records. In this sense, records refers to diary entries – a description of a social interaction, a daily record, and so forth. Faulty records need to be deleted, otherwise analyses will be based on poor data and the results will reflect the classic computing adage of GIGO (Garbage In – Garbage Out). Of course, the number of records that are deleted and the reasons for their deletion need to be recorded.

Generally speaking, researchers do not need to worry about deleting records or about deleting participants. A certain amount of non-compliance is just about inevitable in diary studies. Keep in mind that participants are being asked to provide responses (perhaps numerous responses) over an extended period of time. Even the best of intentions can be overcome by life's vicissitudes. Moreover, the types of analyses that are usually used for diary data can easily accommodate varying numbers of observations for each participant. There is no need to make certain that each participant has the same number of observations.

Finally, deleting all the data for a certain percentage of participants is also quite common, if not inevitable. Attrition and "bad data" rates are higher in diary studies than they are in your typical single assessment study (or at least they have been in my experience). In my research, it has not been uncommon to eliminate 10% of participants (entirely, all their data) from the final analysis. In some cases, participants may provide some valid diary-level data, but I have been reluctant to accept as valid diary-level data that have not been provided on a somewhat consistent basis. I discuss this below.

Of course, if the amount of non-compliance is such that it calls into question the representativeness of the data that are retained, that is another matter. As discussed in the chapter on study design, researchers need to design data collection protocols that participants will follow. Although guarantees are not possible, a sense of how well participants will comply with a protocol can be had via pretesting.

One of the most straightforward decisions about deleting a record that can be made concerns the "time window" during which a record was provided. For example, if a data collection protocol calls for end-of-day reports, what constitutes the end of the day? Such decisions need to be made by researchers themselves, presumably because they are familiar with the lifestyles of the participants. For most people, one can probably assume that the end of the day begins somewhere around 9pm, probably later than this for most people. This would mean that an entry provided at 5pm or 7pm would be deleted. Regardless, I know of no firm norms regarding this in part because data collection protocols and populations vary widely.

For data collected on a daily (or near-daily) basis, reasonable questions can be raised about next day reports. When is it too late for a report provided on day n to be considered as a valid description of what happened on day $n - 1$? I know of no formal rule regarding this, and in published research I have seen (and I have used) 10am of the next morning. Seems sensible to me. Moreover, there are instances in which delayed reports are probably necessary. For example, it is difficult to imagine that participants in a study of sexual activity will complete some type of form immediately following sexual activity. Regardless, researchers need to establish criteria and apply them. See Smith et al. (2007) for an example of such an application.

Noting this, the norms for "beeper studies" and the like seem to be more clearly established. Based upon research discussed by Delespaul (1995), typically, reports are deleted if they are provided more than 15 minutes after the beep signaling the need to report occurs.

After records that fall outside of response windows are deleted, the general pattern of compliance needs to be examined. In some cases, entries that are temporally isolated might be eliminated. For example, assume a participant provides valid data for seven days, then no valid data for three days, then a day of valid data, and then no valid data for the remainder of the study. In such a case, it might be best to delete the isolated single day of data. Who knows why that specific day was recorded when the days before and after it were not?

In some cases, all the remaining records for a participant might be deleted (i.e., the participant is eliminated from the study). One simple rule is based on the number of valid entries a participant has provided. If data collection is meant to occur over two weeks, and a participant provides data for only three days, it seems difficult to assume that the participant has complied with the collection protocol. Moreover, low levels of compliance call into question the validity of the data that were provided.

The foregoing discussion has assumed some type of interval-based data collection in which participants are expected to provide data once a day, twice a day, and so forth. Somewhat different criteria need to be applied when evaluating compliance with an event contingent protocol. When a record is generated by the occurrence of a specific type of event, the number and distribution (across time) of records may vary widely across participants.

For example, participants in the study that was the basis for my dissertation maintained a variant of the RIR, and each participant was interviewed in person following each of four rounds of data collection. When participants were interviewed, the pencil and paper diary forms each participant had completed were available. I distinctly recall inspecting one participant's record and found that she had recorded only one interaction per day. I knew the mean was 4–6 per day, with some participants having many more interactions per day. I asked her directly (but gently) if her record was an accurate description of how socially active she had been during the study, while reminding her that her reward for participating would not change as a function of her answer. We also had other questions in the semi-structured interview that addressed the same issue. She replied to this direct question and to the other questions that, yes, the record was accurate. She had about one social interaction per day. It was quite clear to me that she was telling the truth. Her record was accurate.

When evaluating compliance with an event contingent protocol, researchers need to have some sense of the baseline or typical frequency of the event, and some sense of how much people vary around this baseline. If there is considerable within-person variability (e.g., some days have many target events, some have few) or considerable between-person variability (some people tend to have more events than others), it may be difficult to use the simple frequency with which an event is recorded as an indication of compliance. In such cases (which probably represent the rule rather than the exception), researchers will need to make decisions about compliance on other criteria such as the consistency with which the diary has been maintained. This could include the number of consecutive days the diary has been kept, the regularity of the number of events recorded over the interval of the study, the results of interviews, and so forth.

I should note that one of the most surprising aspects of the data I have collected using variants of the RIR is just how different people are. Some are very active, having many interactions per day, whereas others, like the woman I mentioned above, have relatively few interactions. For some, their interactions involve only a small group of people (irrespective of how active they are per se), whereas others spend time with a much larger number of different people. For some, their interactions are quite regular: they interact with the same people at about the same time most days. For others, there is little regularity in when they interact, even if they interact with a relatively small group of people. Such differences make it difficult to develop some sort of template or standard that can be used to judge if a diary is representative of the social life of a specific participant.

In the early days of using the RIR, we routinely eliminated the first and last days the record was kept under the assumption that during the first day participants were not familiar with the record and during the last day they may not have been motivated to record interactions accurately. I am not certain that such trimming was necessary, but at the time we wanted to be cautious about the quality of the data. Regardless, researchers need to be sensitive to the possibility that participants' motivation to maintain a diary accurately will diminish over time. I will note that I have conducted numerous daily diary and social interaction diary studies. I have compared data collected during the first and second halves of a study (usually the first and second weeks), and I have not found any meaningful differences between the two on a variety of measures.

Finally, for event contingent studies, there is the issue of the length of an event. For example, in a social interaction diary study, participants may record very lengthy interactions such as an interaction beginning at noon and ending at 8pm. In such instances, I recommend breaking the interaction into a series of briefer interactions with all the data (ratings, persons present, etc.) duplicated for the briefer interactions. So, one eight-hour interaction might become two four-hour interactions. In some special instances, such as overnight interactions that probably describe a romantic couple sleeping together, it might be reasonable to break the overnight interaction into one evening interaction and one morning interaction.

Such lengthy interactions are not that common, and in my experience the results of analyses based on the "original" data and the "adjusted" data are indistinguishable. Moreover, the frequency of such interactions can be reduced by emphasizing in the instructions the importance of entering a new/different interaction when some important aspect of an interaction changes. Participants need to be told that when an interaction changes in some way (e.g., a person arrives or what is being done changes), the present interaction needs to be terminated and a new interaction needs to be entered.

Regardless of the data collection protocol, keep in mind that at least for multi-level modeling analyses, the parameter estimates incorporate the fact that the number of level 1 (diary-level) observations may vary across level 2 units of analysis (people). Although other analytic techniques may not take such differences into account per se, as multilevel modeling (MLM) does, it is certainly possible to weight summary measures to take into account the number of observations a participant provided.

5

Multilevel analyses of diary data: An overview

In this chapter, I present a rationale for thinking of the data produced in diary studies within a multilevel context. This includes understanding what the phrase "multilevel" means and understanding the implications for data analysis of the multilevel nature of diary data. In writing this section, I tried to strike a balance between writing for three audiences: those who know about multilevel analysis but do not know much about diary data; those who know about diary data but do not know about multilevel analysis; and those who do not know much about either. I figured that more readers would fall into the second and third categories than into the first category, but I have tried to discuss the topic with all three audiences in mind.

Out of necessity, there is a reasonable amount of detail about how to conduct multilevel analyses, but this chapter is not about multilevel analyses per se. It is about how to use multilevel analyses to test hypotheses within the context of diary studies. For those who want to know about multilevel analyses per se, just a little bit later I present some references that should be helpful.

As you read this chapter and the next, it may be helpful for you to know that I come to and understand multilevel modeling (MLM) primarily as a data analyst, not as a formal modeler. That is, my primary interest is in using MLM to answer the questions I have as a researcher. I am not interested in modeling (MLM or otherwise) per se. Therefore, what is justifiably important to some (e.g., the details of model comparison) may not be as important to me. Know that I have done my utmost to ensure that when I recommend something, it is current best practice. Nevertheless, those of you who are interested in modeling per se are advised to consult other sources.

As should be obvious by now, the data produced by most diary studies are probably best conceptualized as some type of multilevel data structure. In this instance, "multilevel" refers to the fact that in diary studies data are collected simultaneously at multiple levels of analysis. At one level of analysis are diary-level data (occasions in an interval contingent study, events in an event contingent study data), and person-level data constitute the other level of analysis. It is possible for there to be more than two levels of analysis, but for the moment two levels will suffice. Within the nomenclature of multilevel analysis, such data structures are described as "hierarchically nested" or simply nested. At present (and I suspect for some time), some type of multilevel modeling seems to be the best way to examine relationships within such data structures. Other types of analyses may also be appropriate (for different types of questions), and later, in a separate chapter, I discuss one such alternative, the analysis of within-person instability.

Particularly for analysts whose primary experience is analyzing data collected in experimental settings, analyzing the data collected in diary studies can be quite challenging. As I discuss a bit later, the types of OLS (Ordinary Least Squares) ANOVA and regression that form the core of most psychologists' statistical training (with a little structural equation modeling thrown in here and there) do not provide a basis for analyzing the types of data structures that diary studies produce. I have listed below some resources that you may find useful for understanding how to analyze diary-style data using MLM.

I realize that many of the references in this list are to my own work, but few others have published articles in which comprehensive analytical frameworks for analyzing diary data have been proposed or described. Regardless, I have tried to be inclusive. I have not, however, included some classic works on random coefficient models per se, i.e., works that are more about statistics than data analysis. The truly curious will have no difficulty ferreting out such references from the list below. In addition, some of the references I listed in the introductory section (rationales for diary studies) contain discussions of some aspects of analyzing data from diary studies.

- Littell, Milliken, Stroup, and Wolfinger (1996) – a very thorough description (the Bible) of using SAS to conduct random coefficient modeling analyses. Not for the beginner nor the faint of heart. Little attention to diary-style research as we consider it here.
- Kreft and de Leeuw (1998) – a general introduction to MLM, no emphasis on diary research per se.
- Singer (1998) – a brief introduction to using SAS to conduct MLM, some coverage of diary-style data.
- Snijders and Bosker (1999) – a general introduction to MLM, no emphasis on diary research per se.
- Nezlek (2001) – an introduction to and overview of using MLM to analyze interval and event contingent data as discussed here, including a justification for using MLM and some basic principles and techniques.
- Raudenbush and Bryk (2002) – the second edition of the original, Bryk and Raudenbush (1992), which introduced describing the equations for different levels separately. Very thorough, not too much attention to diary research as discussed here. A companion to the HLM program.
- Nezlek (2003) – a discussion of using MLM to analyze social interaction diary data.
- Nezlek (2007a) – a discussion of using MLM to analyze data for personality researchers, with explicit discussion of diary-style research.
- Nezlek (2007b) – a discussion of the types of questions that intensive repeated measures designs (mostly diary-style research) can address, with explicit discussion of MLM analyses of diary-style research.

- Schwartz and Stone (2007) – a detailed discussion of using SAS to conduct MLM of an EMA data set, including a discussion of autocorrelation.
- Nezlek (2011) – the companion volume to the present volume in the Sage series. A comprehensive discussion of MLM, including detailed descriptions of using the HLM program with numerous diary-style data examples.
- West et al. (2011) – a discussion of using MLM to analyze interval contingent data, with a discussion of some advanced topics including model fitting and accounting for temporal trends.

Multiple levels of analysis in diary data

As discussed above, diary studies produce data structures that are inherently multilevel. Within a single study, data are collected at different levels of analysis. Within the nomenclature of multilevel analysis, diary entries (occasions, events, etc.) are thought of as nested within persons, and measures collected at diary level will vary within individuals. Measures that do not change across time (or across diary entries) constitute observations at what is usually referred to as the person level (or between-person level).

Most researchers will be familiar with analyses of person-level measures, which can include what are sometimes referred to as trait or dispositional measures. Participant gender and race are prototypical person-level measures. Neither changes across diary entries. Although some might argue otherwise, personality traits are also typically considered to be a stable, relatively unchanging individual difference. It is possible to model changes across time in person-level measures, a topic addressed below in the section on panel designs.

In contrast, diary-level measures will vary within persons (across diary entries). For example, in a social interaction diary study, how satisfying an individual finds different interactions to be will vary. In a daily diary study, the mood or well-being an individual experiences will vary from day to day. If a diary-level measure does not change, then, de facto, it becomes a person-level measure. For example, in a daily diary study, if some participants have a certain stressful experience every day (e.g., an argument with a spouse) and some never do, then arguing with a spouse becomes a between-person variable. In a social interaction diary study, if people interact only with members of their own sex (e.g., in some type of camp or training group), then there is no variability to examine at the diary level in terms of the sex of co-interactants. Sex of co-interactant becomes a person-level variable, in this case redundant with participant sex. Admittedly, in diary research, these types of situations do not occur that often, but the point is that if there is no variability in a measure at level n, the measure "moves up" to level $n + 1$.

Throughout this volume, I discuss such multiple levels of analysis in terms of separate data sets, person level, diary level, and so forth. To me, this makes the most sense because it helps maintain the distinctions among constructs at different levels of analysis. Nevertheless, keep in mind that different software packages require different data structures to perform MLM, and what are conceptually distinct data sets may need to be merged before conducting analyses.

As I discuss later in the section on nesting and levels of analysis, more than two levels of analysis are possible. For example, in a beeper study, occasions of measurement (beeps) may be nested within days which may then be nested within persons. Persons may also be thought of as nested within "higher" or broader units such as culture. For example, a diary study done in 25 countries would produce a data structure in which days were nested within persons which were nested within countries. For simplicity's sake, I focus primarily on two-level data structures. They are the most common in the literature, and the same principles that guide the analyses of two-level data structures guide the analyses of structures with more levels. I also discuss analyses of three-level models in later sections.

Distinguishing, disentangling, and separating relationships at different levels of analysis in diary data

Within the types of multilevel data structures produced in most diary studies, it is essential to take into account the possibility that the relationship between two constructs at the diary level (within person) is different than the relationship between these same constructs at the between-person level. It is equally essential to take into account the possibility that diary-level relationships vary across persons. I illustrate such possibilities below.

Assume that three people each provide five days of data, and, each day, they describe how anxious and depressed they feel, using a 1–10 scale. Two hypothetical sets of observations are depicted below. In the first data set, the diary-level relationship between the two measures is negative for all three persons, whereas the relationship at the between-person level (the relationship of person-level aggregates) is positive. Moreover, if you ignore the fact that different people provided the daily data and simply correlate the two measures across the 15 daily observations, the correlation is about +.54.

	Negative at the diary level, positive at the person level					
	Person 1		Person 2		Person 3	
Day	Anx.	Dep.	Anx.	Dep.	Anx.	Dep.
1	1	6	3	8	5	10
2	1	6	3	8	5	10
3	2	5	4	7	6	9
4	3	4	5	6	7	8
5	3	4	5	6	7	8
Person-level mean	2	5	4	7	6	9

In this second data set, the diary-level relationship is negative for the first person, zero for the second, and positive for the third. As before, the relationship at the between-person level (the relationship of person-level aggregates) is positive. Moreover, if you ignore the fact that different people provided the daily data and simply correlate the two measures across the 15 daily observations, the correlation is about +.80.

	Varying at the diary level, positive at the person level					
	Person 1		Person 2		Person 3	
Day	Anx.	Dep.	Anx.	Dep.	Anx.	Dep.
1	1	6	3	8	8	10
2	1	6	5	8	8	10
3	2	5	4	7	7	9
4	3	4	3	6	6	8
5	3	4	5	6	6	8
Person-level mean	2	5	4	7	7	9

Although it may not be obvious from these two examples, it is possible to have any type of relationship at the diary level coexisting with any other type of relationship at the person level. Relationships at the two levels of analysis are mathematically independent (e.g., Nezlek, 2001), and perhaps more important, as discussed by Affleck et al. (1999), relationships at these two levels of analysis may represent different psychological processes. Such possibilities beg questions such as: "What is the '*real*' relationship between depressed and anxious mood?" As is so often the case in life, the answer is: "It depends." In terms of the present example, it depends upon whether you are interested in relationships between dispositional tendencies or in more state-like relationships. Do people who tend to be anxious tend to be depressed (the former), or on days when people feel anxious do they also feel depressed (the latter)? Both are perfectly legitimate interests and questions. It is simply the case that the answers to these two questions may differ.

A rationale for using multilevel random coefficient modeling to analyze diary data

There is a consensus among statisticians that the types of multilevel data that are typically collected in diary studies are best analyzed using a class of techniques referred to as multilevel random coefficient modeling or simply multilevel modeling (MLM). In MLM analyses, units of analysis at one level are treated as nested within units of analysis at another. In an event contingent study, events are treated as nested within persons. In a daily diary study, daily records are nested within persons. In a beeper study, occasions of measurement may be nested within days, which can then be nested within persons.

Diary data such as I have been discussing in this volume should *not* be analyzed using some type of OLS technique such as regression, no matter how sophisticated the model being specified. I describe below some of the types of analyses people have used in the past and what is wrong with them, with apologies to all involved. More detailed discussions of the limitations of using OLS techniques to analyze the data collected in diary studies can be found in Nezlek (2001; 2011).

1 Treating diary entries as independent observations in a regression, with or without some kind of code (e.g., dummy codes) representing the participants, with or without person-level variables appended to the diary entries.

Problems: The entries from an individual are not independent, and treating them as if they were violates a basic assumption of OLS analyses. Putting this aside (not a good thing to do), analyses of diary-level data that ignore the fact that diary-level data are from different people confound person- and diary-level variance. As illustrated in the previous section, even though in the first example data set the diary-level relationship between depressed and anxious mood was negative for all three people, when the days were analyzed together, the relationship between the two measures was positive. Even if a series of dummy codes representing individual participants is added (what is sometimes called a least squares dummy analysis, $n - 1$ codes for n participants), this is also no good. Such analyses assume that the relationship between two diary-level measures is exactly the same for all individuals, and such an assumption is not at all tenable. Even if interaction terms are added to allow diary-level relationships to vary between participants, this is wrong because it does not model error properly (more about this later). Adding person-level variables to diary entries to examine relationships involving person-level measures is also flawed. If the number of diary entries becomes the degrees of freedom in the analysis this is inflated, and it is simply wrong in so many other ways.

2 Calculate various within-person summary measures such as means, correlations, or regression coefficients and then use these summary measures in between-person analyses in combination with "true" person-level measures.

Problems: First, I am obliged to note that in the initial work on the RIR, this is how the data were analyzed. In fact, I spent the better part of my last two years or so in graduate school developing the algorithms that were used for the first 10–15 years or so of RIR-based research (Nezlek & Wheeler, 1984). Basically, these algorithms calculated all sorts of within-person aggregates, such as average satisfaction overall, average satisfaction when friends were present, and so forth. With the introduction of MLM (and the encouragement of an editor here and there), I moved on.

Such analyses of aggregates provide important advantages over the regression analyses using the diary entry as the unit of analysis described before. For example, they allow for the possibility that relationships between x and y vary across individuals. Correlations or regression coefficients can be calculated for each person. Moreover, such summary measures can also be weighted by the number of observations and the reliability of the summary measure to account for individual differences in the samples that serve as the basis for the summary measures.

Nevertheless, analyses of aggregates have important limitations, the most important of which is that aggregation-based analyses conceptualize and model error improperly. In a simple daily diary study there are two sampling errors. One is associated with drawing a sample of participants, and the other is associated with drawing a sample of days. By design, OLS analyses are limited to estimating one error term, which, in the case of these aggregation-based analyses, is the error associated with sampling participants. The error associated with the sampling of interactions or days is not part of the analysis.

It is worth noting, however, that the results of analyses of RIR data that rely on aggregate-based means such as I described above (e.g., average satisfaction in interactions) can be quite similar to the results of corresponding MLM analyses. I have analyzed the same data set both ways a few times and compared the results. This similarity reflects the fact that the within-person means are pretty reliable because participants usually describe enough interactions to constitute a good sample. In contrast, the results of aggregation-based analyses of relationships (covariances) can be very different from the results of comparable MLM analyses. This difference reflects the fact that the reliability of a covariance is a joint (multiplicative) function of the reliabilities of the individual measures involved.

The bottom line is to use MLM. It provides a unified, coherent framework within which a wide variety of relationships can be examined and hypotheses tested.

Note that in a separate volume in this series (Nezlek, 2011), I discuss in detail how to conduct multilevel analyses using the program HLM. This discussion includes how to set up data files, use the HLM program, interpret output, and so forth – basically, just about everything one needs to know to perform the types of MLM analyses I discuss here. Moreover, many of the examples I present in this previous volume concern diary data. In the present volume, although there a few instances in which I mention the program, I do not explain MLM in terms of HLM per se. The analyses I describe can be conducted using any software package that can conduct MLM.

In writing the present volume, I did not expect that readers will have read the other volume. Nevertheless, I did not feel comfortable assuming that all readers of this volume would be familiar with all the aspects of MLM with which one should be familiar to analyze diary data. Given this, there is, out of necessity, some duplication (in terms of the topics covered) between the present volume and the volume on MLM per se. There is no duplicated text, and the examples that I use in this volume are different than those used in the MLM volume.

I assume that readers who are familiar with the details of MLM, but understand some aspects, will be able to "pick it up on the way." For those who are not at all familiar with MLM (or know only that it exists), it might be useful to consult in advance (or simultaneously) the other volume I have written as they read this volume. I have written them to complement each other. The other MLM references I listed previously are also good starting points.

The logic of MLM

In describing the logic of MLM, I rely upon the framework introduced by Bryk and Raudenbush (1992), a framework that I believe represents a pedagogical breakthrough. Rather than discuss MLM in terms of a single model (or equation), Bryk and Raudenbush describe how coefficients are "brought up" from one level of analysis to the next. To me, the great advantage of this approach is that it makes very clear exactly what predictors are being entered at what level of analysis. Traditionally, all coefficients for all levels of analysis were presented and discussed in one, sometimes very long and cumbersome, equation. For an example of this, see the section "What to report." This tradition reflects the fact that in MLM, all coefficients are estimated simultaneously, but I find the "single equation" style of presentation to be difficult to follow.

So, for the time being, let us think about separate models for different levels of analysis, recognizing that they are being estimated at the same time. For the most part, I will focus on two-level models such as a daily diary study or social interaction diary study in which observations are treated as nested within persons. Later, I discuss models with more than two levels.

Note that, within the MLM literature, organizing units of analyses, such as people in a diary study, are referred to as "groups." This terminology reflects the origins of MLM, which was initially designed to disentangle individual vs. group-level effects such as those that exist when analyzing students who are in different classes. Using the term "group" does not mean that people are thought of as group members or anything like that.

At the heart of MLM analyses is the separation of variances and relationships at different levels of analysis. For example, if we measure how anxious person j is on day i, we can think of two separate influences on this. One set of influences consists of characteristics of the person, and the other consists of characteristics of the day. To represent these influences, we could set up two equations, one for the day and one for the person. In its simplest form, this would be the following:

Day level $\qquad y_{ij} = \beta_{0j} + r_{ij}$

Person level $\qquad \beta_{0j} = \gamma_{00} + u_{0j}$

In this model, we have j persons measured on i days. Within MLM, the day level can be referred to as level 1, and the person level can be referred to as level 2. For each of these j persons, we estimate a mean anxiety (β_{0j}), and the deviation of each day's anxiety from an individual's mean anxiety is r_{ij}. In turn, these day-level means are analyzed at the person level, where we estimate the grand mean (γ_{00}, the mean of means) and an individual's deviation from this mean is u_{0j}. How much people's anxiety varies across days is the variance of r_{ij}, the error term at the day level, and how much the mean anxiety for people varies across persons is the variance u_{0j} at the person level. Note that such analyses model the sampling error associated with both persons and days. I discuss this in more detail in Nezlek (2011).

A model such as this is called a totally unconditional or null model, and it provides the basic descriptive statistics of multilevel analysis. The sum of the level 1 and level 2 variances is the total variance, which can be used to calculate the intraclass correlation (ICC). The ICC is the ratio of level 2 variance to the total variance. Note that I am discussing the principles of MLM in terms of analyzing continuous outcomes. Analyzing categorical and other non-linear outcomes follows the same logic, but relies upon slightly different procedures. I discuss these later in a separate section.

In MLM, similar to OLS regression, predictors at all levels of analysis can be either continuous or nominal measures. The prototypical continuous measure is a scale of some kind, e.g. (a measure of self-esteem). Scores are meant to represent an observation's place on some type of continuum. Nominal or categorical predictors are measures that represent the category or group into which an observation falls. For example, in daily diary study, a diary-level categorical predictor could be whether the day on which an observation was taken was a weekday or a weekend day. A person-level categorical predictor could be a person's sex.

Predictors can be added to either level of analysis. For example, if you were interested in the relationship between mean daily anxiety and a person-level (trait) variable such as self-esteem, you would include a predictor at the person level. If the γ_{01} coefficient was significant, then you could conclude that daily anxiety was related to self-esteem:

Day level $\qquad y_{ij} = \beta_{0j} + r_{ij}$

Person level $\qquad \beta_{0j} = \gamma_{00} + \gamma_{01}(\text{Self-esteem}) + u_{0j}$

The direction and size of this relationship are indicated by the sign and size of the coefficient. As discussed later in the section on standardizing measures, MLM analyses produce only unstandardized coefficients. I encourage you to get into the habit of thinking of relationships within the MLM framework in terms of pre-dicted or expected values. In terms of the present example, what would the expected daily anxiety be for a person who was +1 SD on trait self-esteem and for someone who was −1 SD? Keep in mind that the γ_{01} coefficient is expressed in raw units, i.e., whatever metric was used to measure trait self-esteem. The coefficient represents the expected change in daily anxiety associated with a 1 unit change in self-esteem. To describe the relationship between trait self-esteem and mean daily anxiety in standard units, the γ_{01} coefficient would need to be divided by the SD of trait self-esteem.

To examine day-level relationships, predictors are added to the day-level model. The model below examines the relationship between daily stress and daily anxiety. In essence, for each person a coefficient is estimated representing this relationship (β_{1j}). The mean of these coefficients is tested for significance at the person level (the γ_{10} coefficient). The hypothesis is that the mean is 0. Note that β_{0j} and β_{1j} are both referred to as coefficients; however, to distinguish them, β_{0j} is called an intercept and β_{1j} is called a slope. Note that each coefficient has its own error term, and how/if these terms are included or not is discussed in a later sec-tion on modeling error.

Day level $\quad\quad y_{ij} = \beta_{0j} + \beta_{1j}(\text{Stress}) + r_{ij}$

Person level $\quad \beta_{0j} = \gamma_{00} + u_{0j}$

$\quad\quad\quad\quad\quad\quad \beta_{1j} = \gamma_{10} + u_{1j}$

Predictors at the person level can be added to this model. In the model below, self-esteem has been added as a predictor of both the intercept (γ_{00}) and the slope (γ_{10}). In essence, the coefficients estimated at the day level (a slope and an inter-cept for each person) are "brought up" to the person level, and individual differ-ences in these coefficients are examined.

Day level $\quad\quad y_{ij} = \beta_{0j} + \beta_{1j}(\text{Stress}) + r_{ij}$

Person level $\quad \beta_{0j} = \gamma_{00} + \gamma_{01}(\text{Self-esteem}) + u_{0j}$

$\quad\quad\quad\quad\quad\quad \beta_{1j} = \gamma_{10} + \gamma_{11}(\text{Self-esteem}) + u_{1j}$

Note that multilevel modelers recommend including the same predictors for all the coefficients being brought up to the next level of analysis, even if person-level relationships are not of interest. This recommendation reflects the fact that all coefficients in a model are estimated simultaneously, based upon covariance matrices. If a predictor is not included (e.g., if self-esteem had not been included as a predictor of the intercept), the model assumes that this coefficient and its covariances with other coefficients are 0. If this assumption is incorrect, the model is misspecified and the parameter estimates may be wrong.

These are the basics of MLM. If you understand what these models represent, you will recognize that all the modeling techniques I discuss in this volume are variations on these basic structures. Frankly, I think many people find MLM confusing because of the difficulties they have using the software. Much MLM software was written for modelers more than for data analysts. Programs provide many options that are simply not of interest to the typical user who has a pile of data and is simply trying to make sense of them. As noted above, in the companion volume to this one, Nezlek (2011), I discuss in detail how to use the program HLM to conduct the types of analyses I describe here. Although HLM was written by some of the world's most respected modelers, I think it can be used by someone who is less interested in modeling per se, but who is more interested in the results of the analyses themselves.

Categorical predictors

Before discussing centering, I need to discuss how categorical predictors can be represented. Categorical predictors can be used at any level of analysis, and the coding schemes I describe here can be applied to predictors at any level of analysis. Categorical measures can be represented with either dummy or contrast codes. Dummy coding is when an observation (e.g., a person) is described in terms of a binary (0 or 1) variable or set of variables. For example, participant sex could be represented by a dummy code indicating if a participant was male or not, coded 1 for men and 0 for women. Sex could also be coded to represent if a participant was a female or not, coded 0 for men and 1 for women. Dummy codes can be used to represent categorical systems with more than two categories. For example, participants' educational level might be represented by three dummy codes: high school only, some college, and college graduate.

As suggested by the name, contrast codes represent comparisons (contrasts) of the specific categories within a categorical system. A contrast code for sex could be 1 for men and −1 for women (or vice versa). A contrast code for education could be 2 for high school, −1 for some college, and −1 for college graduate. This code compares participants who had only a high school degree to those who had more than a high school degree. Moreover, multiple categorical predictor codes can be used simultaneously and can be combined to represent joint classification – see the section on non-intercept models.

Note that the numbers assigned to the specific groups in a contrast code need to sum to 0 (1 and −1; 2, −1, and −1; −3, 1, 1, and 1; etc.) because in MLM coefficients are significance tested against 0. When interpreting results that are based on contrast codes, if the coefficient representing a contrast is significantly different from 0, then the differences among the groups that the contrast represents are significant. As always, a good way to do this is to generate predicted values.

Regardless, it is critically important to keep in mind what exactly the coefficients represent when using categorical predictors (as with all predictors). Take a daily diary study in which positive affect is the dependent measure and weekday–weekend differences are of interest. In the first equation, Weekday is a dummy code, 1 = weekday, 0 = weekend day. In the second equation, Day-type is a contrast code, 1 = weekday, −1 = weekend day.

Day level $\quad y_{ij} = \beta_{0j} + \beta_{1j}(\text{Weekday}) + r_{ij}$

Day level $\quad y_{ij} = \beta_{0j} + \beta_{1j}(\text{Day-type}) + r_{ij}$

Assuming the two predictors are centered in the same way (next section), the significance tests of two slopes from these two equations will be the same; however, the intercepts can differ. For example, and as explained next, if the predictors are entered uncentered (the standard for categorical predictors), the intercept in the first equation will represent the mean positive affect for weekends (when weekday = 0). In contrast, the intercept in the second equation will represent the mean positive affect on a day that is neither a weekend day nor a weekday. Admittedly, such days do not exist, but in this case the intercept comes closest to the intercept from an unconditional model, which may be desirable because this also means that the error structure is closer to the unconditional model. See Enders and Tofighi (2007) for a discussion of this issue.

Centering

For analysts whose primary experience is with OLS regression, one of the challenging aspects of MLM can be what is called "centering." Centering refers to the reference value that is used to estimate the relationships between a predictor and an outcome. In OLS regression, this is invariably the mean. For example, a correlation represents how well, for a sample of observations, deviations of a variable x from its mean correspond to (or predict) deviations of a variable y from its mean. In OLS regression, if one is interested in standardized coefficients, the intercept is virtually meaningless. In contrast, in MLM, how variables are centered and the implications of centering for what coefficients mean (both slopes and intercepts) are critical. The meaning of coefficients will vary as a function of how predictors are centered, and different centering options can produce coefficients that are meaningfully different from each other. See Enders and Tofighi (2007) and Nezlek (2011) for a discussion of centering within MLM, and see Nezlek (2001; 2003) for discussions of centering within diary studies specifically.

At the person level, level 2 in a two-level diary data set, there are two centering options, grand-mean centered and uncentered. Note that uncentered is sometimes referred to as zero centered. When a predictor is entered uncentered, the reference point is 0, and the intercept is the expected value for someone who has a score of 0 on that predictor. This is equivalent to the standardized coefficients in OLS regression. When a predictor is grand-mean centered, the grand mean becomes the "reference point" for a predictor (the value from which deviations are calculated), and the intercept represents the expected value for an observation (person) at the mean of a predictor. This is equivalent to the unstandardized coefficients in OLS regression.

Deciding how to center person-level predictors is relatively straightforward. Typically, continuous measures are entered grand-mean centered, similar to standardized coefficients in OLS regression. Assume the following analysis of daily self-esteem. The person-level variable, CESD, stands for Center for Epidemiological Studies Depression scale, a widely used measure of depressive symptoms (Radloff, 1977).

Day level $\quad y_{ij} = \beta_{0j} + r_{ij}$

Person level $\quad \beta_{0j} = \gamma_{00} + \gamma_{01}(\text{CESD}) + u_{0j}$

If CESD scores were entered grand-mean centered, then the intercept, γ_{00}, would represent the expected daily self-esteem score for someone who was at the mean of the CESD. The slope, γ_{01}, would represent the change in daily self-esteem associated with a 1 unit change in CESD scores. A positive slope would indicate that self-esteem increases as CESD scores increase, a negative slope would indicate that self-esteem decreases as CESD scores increase. By the way, the slope in such an analysis is invariably negative. Daily self-esteem, like trait self-esteem, is negatively related to reports of depressive symptoms.

If CESD scores were entered uncentered, then the intercept, γ_{00}, would represent the expected daily self-esteem score for someone who had a score of 0 on the CESD. Similar to the grand-mean centered analysis, the slope, γ_{01}, would represent the change in daily self-esteem associated with a 1 unit change in CESD scores, and the sign of the slope is interpreted similarly. Note that if CESD scores are standardized prior to analysis, grand-mean centering and zero centering will produce exactly the same coefficients because the grand mean of a standardized measure is 0. Also, entering a predictor uncentered when 0 is not a valid value for that predictor is not recommended because the analysis uses a non-existent value as a reference point.

The same centering options are available for categorical predictors, and the two options function in the same way. Given their nature, however, a brief explanation of how they work is probably best. Most modelers recommend entering categorical predictors uncentered because this makes it easier to interpret the coefficients than when they are grand-mean centered. Assume the following analysis of intimacy in social interaction. The person-level variable, Female, is a dummy-coded variable, 1 for women, 0 for men:

Interaction level $\quad y_{ij} = \beta_{0j} + r_{ij}$

Person level $\quad\quad \beta_{0j} = \gamma_{00} + \gamma_{01}(\text{Female}) + u_{0j}$

If Female is entered uncentered, then the intercept, γ_{00}, would represent the expected intimacy in interaction for men, i.e., for participants for whom Female = 0. The slope, γ_{01}, would represent the difference between men and women. The expected score for a woman would be $\gamma_{00} + \gamma_{01}*1$. If Female is entered grand-mean centered, then the intercept would represent the expected score for someone who was at the mean score on Female. Given that Female is a dichotomous measure, no person could be at the mean, but the intercept has the value of representing the sample mean adjusted for the distribution of men and women – something that will become more useful when considering centering at level 1. The slope represents the sex difference, and although the specific value of the coefficient will differ from the coefficient when Female is entered uncentered, the results of the significance test will be the same. Contrast codes (e.g., men = 1, women = −1), can also be used as predictors. If such a contrast code is entered uncentered, then the intercept represents the expected value for an observation that has a value of 0 – sort of a neutral observation. If it is entered grand-mean centered, then the intercept will represent the sample mean adjusted for the distribution of men and women.

When there are more than two categories for a predictor, the same procedures can be followed. One just needs to keep in mind what the intercepts and coefficients represent. For example, if a 2, −1, −1 contrast code is entered uncentered, the intercept will represent a neutral value, and the slope will be a significance test of the contrast. The sign of the slope will indicate the direction of the difference. For a 2, −1, −1 code, a positive slope would indicate that the estimated score for individuals in the first category was greater than the estimated score for individuals in categories 2 and 3 (averaged). A negative slope would indicate the reverse. In a later section, "No intercept models," I discuss different ways of analyzing group data that provide a basis for comparing groups, and we will return to this issue then.

At the diary level (level 1), and at intermediate levels in models with more than two levels, predictors can be centered in one of three ways: uncentered, grand-mean centered, and group-mean centered. Moreover, how diary-level predictors are centered is typically more important to an analysis than how person-level predictors are centered because diary-level coefficients are brought up to the person level. The meaning of a set of coefficients varies as a function of how predictors are centered. Consequently, what is brought up to and analyzed at the person level will vary as a function of how diary-level predictors are centered. Assume a daily diary study with a diary (day) level predictor Stress. The dependent measure is anxiety.

Day level $\quad y_{ij} = \beta_{0j} + \beta_{1j}(\text{Stress}) + r_{ij}$

Person level $\quad \beta_{0j} = \gamma_{00} + u_{0j}$

$\qquad\qquad\qquad \beta_{1j} = \gamma_{10} + u_{1j}$

Similar to centering at the person level, when a diary-level predictor is entered uncentered, the intercept represents the expected value when the predictor is 0. In the present case, this would be the expected anxiety on totally stress-free days (Stress = 0). When a diary-level predictor is entered grand-mean centered, the intercept represents the expected value when the predictor is at the grand mean of the sample. In the present case, this would be the expected anxiety on a day when Stress was at the mean calculated for the entire sample – all days across all persons. Finally, when a diary-level predictor is entered group-mean centered, the intercept represents the expected value when the predictor is at the mean within each level 2 unit. In the present case, this would be the expected anxiety on a day when Stress was at the mean for each person, which would simply be the mean anxiety for that person. By the way, this is the same as the intercept from a totally unconditional model.

If you want your MLM analyses to be as close to possible as "two-step" regression – conducting a regression analysis for each person and then using the coefficients in a person-level analysis – then you should group-mean center your predictors. When diary-level predictors are group-mean centered, individual differences in predictors do not contribute to parameter estimates. Within our example, if Stress were entered group-mean centered, the Stress slope would be controlled for mean differences in how much stress participants experienced. In addition, if you are going to use changes in variance estimates to estimate effect sizes, predictors need to be group-mean centered. See later section on effect sizes.

Although numerous modelers recommend group-mean centering continuous predictors (e.g., Enders & Tofighi, 2007; Nezlek, 2011), some modelers are concerned that by taking group (person) level differences out of a model, a model excludes valuable information. The proposed remedy for this is to include, as a predictor in the level 2 equations, the mean of any predictor that has been group-mean centered. See West et al. (2011) for a discussion. In my own research, I have not done this when using group-mean-centered predictors in part because the relationships including this coefficient estimate were not of particular interest.

In contrast, entering diary-level predictors grand-mean centered moves level 2 (person-level) variance of a predictor to level 1 (diary level), and there may be instances in which this is desirable. For example, assume a social interaction diary study with a diary (interaction) level predictor Dyad, coded 1 for dyads and 0 for non-dyads. The dependent measure is intimacy.

Interaction level $\quad y_{ij} = \beta_{0j} + \beta_{1j}(\text{Dyad}) + r_{ij}$

Person level $\quad\quad \beta_{0j} = \gamma_{00} + u_{0j}$

$\quad\quad\quad\quad\quad\quad \beta_{1j} = \gamma_{10} + u_{1j}$

If Dyad were entered grand-mean centered, the intercept would represent the average intimacy a person experienced in interaction, *adjusted for between-person differences in the percentage of interactions that were dyads*. The adjustment is due to the fact that the intercept represents the expected value for an interaction that is at the grand mean of dyads, which takes into account differences between people in how many dyadic interactions they had. Such adjustments can be quite valuable, and I discuss such issues in a later section on statistical controls.

Overall recommendations are as follows. In general, enter categorical predictors uncentered – this keeps the meaning of the intercept clear. In general, enter continuous measures grand-mean centered at the person level and group-mean centered at the diary level. Finally, when thinking of centering the predictors in your analyses, I recommend keeping Bryk and Raudenbush (1992: 27) in mind: "No single rule covers all cases." You will need to make decisions based upon the structure of your data and the questions in which you are interested. Moreover, by combining different ways of coding predictors with different centering options, a variety of specific relationships can be examined. I discuss some of these combinations in later sections.

Modeling error

A critical aspect of MLM is specifying the error terms, which, taken as a collective, are sometimes referred to as the error structure. Modeling error in MLM is very different from modeling error in OLS analyses. In OLS analyses, there is only one error term for each level of a model, and these error terms are estimated separately. For example, in an ANOVA with between and within factors, there are separate error terms for the within and between parts of the design. In contrast, in MLM, each coefficient has (or can have) a separate error term, and these error terms, and the covariances between them, are estimated simultaneously. In this volume, I have tried to discuss the more important points of modeling error within the context of diary studies. Readers who thirst for more are advised to consult Nezlek (2011) and the other MLM references listed in the Introduction. In addition, I discuss autocorrelation (a hot topic in diary research) in a separate section later.

To me, modeling errors in MLM is a bit paradoxical. On the one hand, error structures need to be specified properly, otherwise you can have a "misspecified" model that can lead to inaccurate significance tests. Keep in mind that all parameters (all coefficients and error terms and all the covariances) are estimated simultaneously in MLM, so a weakness in one part of the model can spill over into other parts. Okay, it is important to model error properly. On the other hand, rarely do hypotheses concern error terms or structures per se. Hypotheses in diary research invariably concern some type of fixed effect. Are two daily measures related? Does some person-level measure moderate such a relationship? Such questions are answered by testing fixed effects, not by testing error terms.

The analogy that I use when giving MLM workshops is that the error structure of a model is like the foundation of a house, whereas fixed effects are the rooms in the house. If the foundation is no good, who cares what the rooms themselves are like? On the other hand, few people buy a house because it has a good foundation. They are attracted by the rooms themselves. Few readers will find your study interesting because of how you modeled error per se. Most readers will be interested in the substantive conclusions you reach, which, almost all of the time, will be based upon tests of fixed effects; however, some readers may be suspicious of the substantive conclusions you reach if they believe that you did not model error properly.

As explained earlier, in a diary study, units at each level of analysis constitute samples from their respective populations, and error terms are estimated at each level of analysis. In a daily diary study in which some daily measure such as positive affect is modeled as a function of daily positive events and negative events (as below), there are four error terms: the day-level error, r_{ij}, and an error term for each of the three coefficients being brought up to the person level (u_{0j}, u_{1j}, and u_{2j}). Note that the term "random variance," and sometimes "random effect," refers to the variance of these terms.

Day level $\quad\quad\quad y_{ij} = \beta_{0j} + \beta_{1j}(\text{PosEvent}) + \beta_{2j}(\text{NegEvent}) + r_{ij}$

Person level $\quad\quad \beta_{0j} = \gamma_{00} + u_{0j}$

$\quad\quad\quad\quad\quad\quad \beta_{1j} = \gamma_{10} + u_{1j}$

$\quad\quad\quad\quad\quad\quad \beta_{2j} = \gamma_{20} + u_{2j}$

Within MLM, γ coefficients (level 2 coefficients) have two components: a fixed effect and a random effect. The fixed effect is an estimate of the mean coefficient in the population, and the random effect is an estimate of the random variation of that effect in the population. Most hypotheses concern fixed effects, e.g., is the relationship between positive events and positive affect different from 0 (the γ_{10} coefficient in the above model)? The random effect is also tested. Do the data provide the information needed to estimate the random error – to separate true and random variability?

Theoretically, I think coefficients in diary studies are best conceptualized as random, the error terms in the above level 2 equations. The diary entries (days in this example) and the persons have been sampled from their respective populations. A different sample of days would have provided slightly different estimates of coefficients, and this variance needs to be taken into account. The same can be said for virtually any diary study. By the way, I am not at all convinced by the arguments of researchers who say they are not interested in how slopes vary, as an attempt to justify not modeling the random terms. Such nonsense is common in some research areas such as economics. It is easy to model (or to try to model) the random variability of a slope. Simply because you believe that slopes do not vary or you are not interested in whether they do, does not justify conducting an analysis that assumes something is the case that may not be the case and can be tested empirically.

Moving past this issue, the critical issue is whether the data provide a basis for estimating these error terms (and their covariances). Although there is not a true consensus about this, many (perhaps most) multilevel modelers recommend deleting non-significant random error terms. The rationale for this is that there is no reason to use data to estimate a parameter that cannot be estimated reliably. Regardless, given the importance of modeling random variability, most multilevel modelers recommend using a more relaxed p-value for making decisions about including random error terms. The norm is to include error terms if the p-value is .10 or less, and drop them if the p-value is greater than .15. What about error terms for which the p-value is between .10 and .15? In such cases, I recommend running the models with and without the error terms and seeing if tests of the fixed effects vary. If they do not, the issue is typically moot. If they do, you will have to make an informed decision about which model best represents the data. This can be done by comparing the overall model fits.

In my opinion, interpreting the significance of error terms is one of the most misunderstood aspects of MLM. To provide a context for considering this issue, I note that coefficients can be modeled in one of three ways:

1 Randomly varying – a fixed effect and a random effect are estimated for a coefficient. In terms of the nomenclature used to describe models, these are the γ and u terms in the model above. Level 2 predictors can also be added.
2 Fixed – only a fixed effect is estimated; no u (error) terms and no level 2 predictors.
3 Non-randomly varying – only a fixed effect is estimated; no u terms, but there are level 2 predictors.

I believe a source of confusion is that if a random error term is not (or cannot be) estimated for a coefficient, analysts often assume that this means there is no variance in the coefficients. In a limited sense, this is true. If a random term is not estimated for a coefficient, the random variability is not being estimated. Moreover, in some programs, if you request estimated coefficients (e.g., what are called residual files in HLM), all participants will have the same estimated coefficient if a random effect is not estimated for a coefficient.

Nevertheless, the fixed variance is estimated, and this is used to estimate the standard error that is used for significance testing. A non-significant random error term simply means that the data have not provided the basis to separate true (fixed) and random variability – no more, no less. The absence of a significant random effect does not preclude the possibility of modeling the fixed variance. One way to understand this is to include a level 2 (person-level) predictor for a slope for which no random error term has been estimated. When you examine the estimated values for this coefficient, you will see that they do vary as a function of the level 2 predictor.

The bottom line is, if your hypotheses of interest concern individual differences in diary-level relationships, you can (and should) include these individual differences in your model irrespective of whether you estimate a random error term for the slopes representing these relationships.

Building models in MLM

In MLM, building a model refers to how an analyst decides what predictors to include and what types of error term will be included for each coefficient. Although there are no rigid laws about how to build models in MLM, there are some widely accepted guidelines that can help diary researchers analyze their data. First, and seemingly unimportant, analysts should run unconditional models (no predictors at any level of analysis) for the variables that are the primary focus of the analyses, both outcomes and predictors. Such analyses provide the basic descriptive statistics of multilevel data – the mean and variance estimates for different levels of analysis. In your prototypical two-level diary study, unconditional models estimate the mean and the diary- and person-level variances. By the way, these are sometimes called "null" models because there are no predictors.

Although the results of unconditional models typically do not test hypotheses per se (unless there is some interest in knowing if a mean score is different from 0), they do provide two types of information. First, they provide a context within which the tests of hypotheses can be better understood. What are the data like? Second, the variance estimates may provide some type of guidance about "where the action is" in a measure – at the diary level, person level, or both. At what level of analysis can relationships be found? If there is little or no variance at a level of analysis, it may be difficult to model relationships at that level of analysis. In my experience, *most* diary-level measures have reasonable distributions of variances, allowing analyses at both the diary and person levels. Note the italics.

In Nezlek, Kafetsios, and Smith (2008a), we studied emotion in social interaction using a social interaction diary. The primary focus of the study was the relationship between person-level measures of self-construal and interaction-level measures of emotion. As expected, we found numerous relationships between self-construal and positive emotions, but we found very few relationships between construal and negative emotions. In early drafts of the manuscript, we kept trying to explain why this was so. If we had followed the advice I just gave and looked at the variance estimates of unconditional models, we would have seen that for measures of negative emotions, there was very little variance at the person level. In contrast, for measures of positive emotion, there was ample variance at the person level. We could not model person-level differences in negative emotions because there was simply not that much person-level variance in these measures to model. It was very embarrassing for me to find this out after we had tried to explain the lack of relationships from a theoretical perspective.

As a general norm, multilevel modelers recommend building models up rather than down. Lower level models should be finalized before adding predictors to upper level models. For diary researchers, this means finalizing diary-level models before adding person-level moderators. In this context, "finalizing" refers to the selection and centering of predictors and modeling error. Build a solid day-level model, then see and examine individual differences in this model. If there are intermediate levels (e.g., days), models at these levels should be finalized before moving up. For example, in a three-level "beeper study" in which beeps are nested within days and days are nested within persons, the beep-level model is set, then the day-level model, and then the person-level model.

Note that it is possible that the significance tests of error terms change when person-level predictors are added to an analysis. If you have finalized your diary-level model before doing this, the only change you will be able to see is when a significant error term becomes non-significant. (This presumes that you have eliminated the error terms that could not be estimated reliably before adding person-level predictors.) In such cases, it is not clear what to do – keep the term based on the initial diary-level models, or delete them given that they are no longer significant. To understand fully what is going on, I recommend comparing the fixed effects (usually the focus of hypotheses) estimated with and without the random error term. If the fixed effects do not change, then you can keep or delete the term without any concerns. If the fixed effects do change, then you need to decide which model to retain. This can be done by testing the overall fit of the model, similar to what is done in structural equation modeling (SEM). In my experience, rarely has including or excluding error terms *under such circumstances* made a difference in terms of the tests of fixed effects, but your experience may be different.

The next issue is adding predictors. The norm here is very clear: use forward stepping rather than backward stepping algorithms. Forward stepping is when you start with a basic (null) model, add predictors slowly, often one at a time, and evaluate your models as each predictor is added. In contrast, backward stepping is when you start with a group of predictors, delete predictors (sometimes one at a time), and evaluate your models as each predictor is deleted. Backward stepping is used in many OLS settings. Part of the rationale for this is that including all the predictors simultaneously controls for the covariances among predictors and permits the inclusion of control variables.

Putting aside whether backward stepping is the best way to examine relationships within OLS, it is clearly not the best way to build models in MLM, particularly at the within-person (diary) level. The reason for this is the number of parameters that are estimated in MLM. In OLS, the intercept is estimated, a fixed effect is estimated for each predictor, and one error term is estimated. In MLM, for each predictor both a fixed effect and an error term are estimated, and the covariances between the errors are also estimated. As predictors are added to a model, the number of parameters increases non-linearly, more easily taxing what some call the "carrying capacity" of the data – the ability of a data set to estimate parameters. I illustrate this below.

In a two-level diary study, in an unconditional model, three parameters are estimated: a level 1 variance, and fixed and random effects for the intercept. If a single level 1 predictor is added, six parameters are estimated: the level 1 variance, a fixed and random effect for the intercept, a fixed and random effect for the first predictor, and the covariance between the two random effects. If a second predictor is added, 10 parameters are estimated: the level 1 variance, a fixed and random effect for the intercept and the two slopes, and the covariances between the three random effects.

Unless you have a lot of diary-level entries and a lot of participants, you will not be able to estimate all these parameters if you include a bunch of predictors simultaneously. You will know (or suspect) this is the case if you have trouble estimating random effects when predictors are analyzed together, whereas you had no trouble estimating these effects when the predictors were entered individually. Certainly there may be times when you will need to include a certain group of diary-level predictors in a single analysis. Nevertheless, you need to keep in mind that the norm in MLM is to have tighter, more parsimonious models with fewer predictors rather than bloated models that stretch or exceed the ability of a data set to estimate coefficients reliably.

The foregoing has focused on the number of diary-level predictors. The same types of problems do not occur when adding person-level (level 2) predictors. This is because of the way in which error is modeled. Level 2 predictors do not each get their own error term and so forth. Nevertheless, I encourage you to think about building tight and parsimonious person-level models at level 2 also. Less is often more.

Interactions, moderation, and mediation

In discussing moderation and mediation, I will rely upon the classic distinction initially offered by Baron and Kenny (1986). Moderation occurs when the relationship between two variables varies as a function of a third variable. In contrast, mediation occurs when the relationship between two variables can be explained by a third variable. For diary-style data, moderation can occur both within levels of analysis and between levels of analysis. Moreover, moderation is best considered as a type of interaction.

Within your typical diary study, interactions can occur both between and within levels. We have already covered cross-level interactions, when a diary level (within-person relationship) varies as a function of a person-level variable. This is also sometimes called a moderating relationship. The person-level variable is said to moderate the diary-level relationship. Such moderators can be categorical or continuous.

Interactions can also exist within a level of analysis and can be used to determine if a variable moderates a relationship between two other variables measured at the same level of analysis. In discussing how to set up these analyses, I follow the advice of Aiken and West (1991), a valuable resource. Within a regression framework, interactions are tested by a term consisting of the product of two measures. Continuous predictors should be centered before doing this. Decisions about how to represent categorical predictors (contrast or dummy codes) need to take into account the specific relationships that are of interest. See the previous section on categorical predictors.

It is somewhat simpler to examine moderating relationships at the person level than at the diary level. For example, assume a social interaction diary study, and the dependent measure is intimacy. In the following model, the possibility that participant sex moderates the relationship between CESD and mean intimacy of interaction is tested by the γ_{03} term. Assuming that CESD scores were centered before creating the interaction term, I would enter the sex contrast variable uncentered, the CESD term grand-mean centered, and the interaction term uncentered. If this term is significant, the exact nature of the interaction (the moderating relationship) can be understood by generating predicted values for men and women high and low on the CESD. As discussed in the later section on standardizing measures, this can be made a lot easier by standardizing CESD scores before doing anything. This interaction could also have been tested by using two dummy codes (one for men, one for women), multiplying CESD scores by each of these dummy codes, dropping the intercept, entering all four predictors uncentered, and then comparing the two interaction terms (γ_{02} and γ_{04}) in the alternative model below. More details about such models are provided in the section on no-intercept models. Examining an interaction between two continuous measures is done in a similar fashion, albeit by using two centered measures to create the interaction term.

Interaction level $y_{ij} = \beta_{0j} + r_{ij}$

Person level $\beta_{0j} = \gamma_{00} + \gamma_{01}(\text{SexCnt}) + \gamma_{02}(\text{CESD}) + \gamma_{03}(\text{Sex*CESD}) + u_{0j}$

Alternative model $\beta_{0j} = \gamma_{01}(\text{Male}) + \gamma_{02}(\text{Male*CESD}) + \gamma_{03}(\text{Female})$
$+ \gamma_{04}(\text{Female*CESD}) + u_{0j}$

Finally, slopes as well as intercepts can be examined with such analyses. For example, if a person-level variable moderated a within-person relationship, the possibility that this moderating relationship is moderated by another person-level variable can be examined using the same analysis as that just presented. One simply adds the appropriate person-level predictors to the person-level model for the slope representing the within-person relationship.

Examining moderation at the diary level follows the same principles as just described. The essential difference is that when examining interactions involving continuous predictors, the predictors need to be centered within each person. This entails subtracting a person's mean for a predictor from each of that person's observations for that predictor. Interaction terms and categorical predictors are entered uncentered, and continuous predictors are entered group-mean centered. One can also use the type of dummy-coded, no-intercept model illustrated above, with all predictors entered uncentered.

Interpreting a significant diary-level interaction is also bit more complicated than interpreting a person-level interaction. First, keep in mind that the person-level coefficient (the γ) for the interaction term represents the mean inter-action. This term, and the nature of the interaction itself, can vary as a function of person-level variables. Second, when generating predicted values for observations that are ±1 SD on continuous predictors, one needs to use the within-person SD for a predictor. This is estimated by an unconditional model of the predictor. When interactions involve only categorical predictors, estimated values can be generated simply by "plugging in" the appropriate values for the categories.

Space does not permit a more detailed explanation of how to do this. You can find examples of analyses of diary-level interactions including person-level moderators of these interactions in Nezlek and Plesko (2003) and Nezlek and Allen (2006). Moreover, a full explanation of how to do such analyses, including a description of how to estimate predicted values to interpret diary-level interactions that are moderated by person-level variables, can be found in Nezlek (2011).

Evaluating mediation is meaningfully more complex than evaluating moderation and is an area that is evolving as I write this volume (literally). The most recent strategy I could find involves using multilevel SEM (MSEM), but a detailed discussion of this approach is well beyond the scope of this volume. If you must know more, consult Preacher, Zyphur, and Zhang (2010) for an introduction. It will suffice to note that the MSEM approach provides a basis for testing a wider variety of mediational relationships than the MLM approach, although my reading of this approach suggests that variables need to be measured with more than one item, which may limit its application. Moreover, it was not clear to me that the technique can be applied to examining mediational relationships between predictors at the person level of slopes brought up from the diary level. I am certain this issue will be addressed in the future.

When thinking of mediation, an analyst (you) must be certain what type of mediation is being examined. The nomenclature for multilevel mediation involves 2s and 1s, denoting level 2 (person-level) and level 1 (diary-level) variables respectively. So, a 1→1→1 model would represent a situation in which a level 1 variable mediates the relationship between two other level 1 variables, what I will refer to as within-level mediation. An example of this would be if anxiety mediated the relationship between stress and self-esteem in a daily diary study. A 2→2→1 model would be when a level 2 variable mediates the relationship between a level 2 predictor and a level 1 coefficient. I think this is also best conceptualized as within-level mediation because the mediation of the model is occurring within level 2. An example of this would be if depression mediated the relationship between trait social anxiety and interaction satisfaction in a social interaction diary study.

There are numerous other types of mediational relationships that can be conceptualized within a multilevel structure, but I do not have the space here to discuss all of them. It may suffice to note that an important advantage of the MSEM approach that Preacher et al. (2010) advocate is the ability to predict level 2 coefficients from level 1 coefficients. For example, how might a level 1 construct lead to a change in a level 2 construct, which then leads to a change in another level construct, a 1→2→1 model?

Okay, but what does someone do? Learn MSEM to do what may be an analysis of secondary importance? Perhaps. At this point, my recommendation (for within-level mediation) is to start simply. If you have a significant relationship between two variables that becomes non-significant when a second predictor is added, and the second predictor is significant, you have a prima facie case for mediation. If the change in significance levels and size of the coefficient of the original predictor are large, you can feel more confident that mediation has, in fact, occurred. Note that this procedure does not allow for examining partial mediation. But to me, partial mediation has never been very interesting anyway – just one man's opinion.

Bauer, Preacher, and Gil (2006) proposed a different procedure for examining mediation at the diary level. The technique involves some rather tricky data manipulation, which I cannot describe here. I have described it in detail with a fully worked example in Nezlek (2011: 41–44). It might seem to be a bit daunting at first, but if you follow the example I provide, it is eminently practical.

Comparing coefficients, or comparing fixed effects

To me, one of the underutilized aspects of MLM in the analysis of diary data is the ability to compare coefficients (fixed effects). Such comparisons can involve any number and combination of coefficients. The underlying technique is simple.

Coefficients can be compared by examining the impact on the fit of a model of constraining coefficients to be equal. Exactly how such constraints are tested varies across MLM software, and I provide a detailed description of how to test such constraints using the program HLM in Nezlek (2011). The constraint is tested for significance by a chi-square, and the degrees of freedom of the chi-square are equal to the number of comparisons represented in the constraint. I provide examples of this technique in this section, and you will see that this technique is integral to numerous types of analyses I discuss in later sections.

Assume a daily diary study in which self-esteem is the dependent measure and two types of stressors, social and achievement failures/problems, are the predictors. The model would look like the following:

Day level $y_{ij} = \beta_{0j} + \beta_{1j}(\text{Social}) + \beta_{2j}(\text{Achievement}) + r_{ij}$

Person level $\beta_{0j} = \gamma_{00} + u_{0j}$

$\beta_{1j} = \gamma_{10} + u_{1j}$

$\beta_{2j} = \gamma_{20} + u_{2j}$

The strength of the within-person relationships between self-esteem and these two types of events can be compared by constraining the γ_{10} and γ_{20} coefficients to be equal. Such a constraint could take the form of assigning a 1 to the Social slope and -1 to the Achievement slope. If constraining these coefficients to be equal results in a poorer fitting model, then the slopes are not equal. For example, assume the Social slope was $-.54$ and the Achievement slope was $-.35$. The constraint would test if $(1 * -.54) + (-1 * -.35)$, i.e., $-.19$, was significantly different from 0.

Constraints can involve combinations of coefficients and multiple comparisons. Assume daily self-esteem is the dependent measure, and three types of stressors are measured: friends, family, and strangers. The model is as below:

Day level $y_{ij} = \beta_{0j} + \beta_{1j}(\text{Friend}) + \beta_{2j}(\text{Family}) + \beta_{3j}(\text{Stranger}) + r_{ij}$

Person level $\beta_{0j} = \gamma_{00} + u_{0j}$

$\beta_{1j} = \gamma_{10} + u_{1j}$

$\beta_{2j} = \gamma_{20} + u_{2j}$

$\beta_{3j} = \gamma_{30} + u_{3j}$

The following table contains some examples of using constraints to test differences among these three slopes. Comparison C1, a 1 df test, compares the average of the Friend and Family slopes to the Stranger slope. C2 is a 2 df test of the equality of all three slopes. It is conceptually similar to the F-test in an ANOVA with three groups. Similar to an F-ratio with three groups, the test does not indicate which particular slopes are different from each other. You just know that the three of them are not the same.

Slope		C1	C2	
Friend	γ_{10}	1	1	0
Family	γ_{20}	1	0	1
Stranger	γ_{30}	-2	-1	-1

These examples have concerned testing the equality of mean slopes brought up from the day level to the person level; however, constraints can concern coefficients in the same person-level equation. Assume a social interaction diary study in which satisfaction with interactions is the dependent measure. The person-level predictors are depression and social anxiety. The strength of the person-level relationships between satisfaction and these two dispositional measures can be compared by constraining the γ_{01} and γ_{02} coefficients to be equal.

Interaction level $\quad y_{ij} = \beta_{0j} + r_{ij}$

Person level $\quad \beta_{0j} = \gamma_{00} + \gamma_{01}(\text{Depression}) + \gamma_{02}(\text{Social Anxiety}) + u_{0j}$

It is also possible to compare coefficients across person-level equations. Assume a social interaction study and that satisfaction is the dependent measure, the interaction-level predictors are perceived intimacy and control in the interaction, and the person-level predictors are depression and social anxiety. Conceptually, this is an analysis of the correlates of satisfaction in interaction and individual differences in these correlates.

Interaction level $\quad y_{ij} = \beta_{0j} + \beta_{1j}(\text{Intimacy}) + \beta_{2j}(\text{Control}) + r_{ij}$

Person level $\quad \beta_{0j} = \gamma_{00} + \gamma_{01}(\text{Depression}) + \gamma_{02}(\text{Social Anxiety}) + u_{0j}$

$\quad\quad\quad\quad\quad\quad \beta_{1j} = \gamma_{10} + \gamma_{11}(\text{Depression}) + \gamma_{12}(\text{Social Anxiety}) + u_{1j}$

$\quad\quad\quad\quad\quad\quad \beta_{2j} = \gamma_{20} + \gamma_{21}(\text{Depression}) + \gamma_{22}(\text{Social Anxiety}) + u_{2j}$

For example, the hypothesis that social anxiety moderates the relationship between intimacy and satisfaction more strongly than it moderates the relationship between control and satisfaction can be tested by constraining the γ_{12} and γ_{22} coefficients to be equal. This example is intended to illustrate the point that any γ coefficient can be compared to any other γ coefficient. The key is to set up your models so that the γ coefficients represent psychologically meaningful entities. That is the hard part. Comparing them is the easy part.

All of the previous examples have involved comparisons of coefficients that were the same sign: all positive or all negative. There may be times, however, when you want to compare the strength of coefficients, irrespective of their signs. Such comparisons are suggested by the general idea that negative stimuli are more influential than positive stimuli. To understand how to make such comparisons, it is instructive to recognize that, conceptually, constraints test if some type of weighted sum is different from 0. For example, the comparison of the social and achievement slopes in the previous example tested whether the sum of (1 * −.54) and (−1 * −.35) was different from 0.

I suspect that when most researchers think of these types of constraints, some type of contrast coding comes to mind. Nevertheless, there may be times when contrast codes do not represent comparison of interest, e.g., when hypotheses concern the absolute size (magnitude) of effects that are of different signs. Assume a daily diary study in which the outcome is daily self-esteem and the two predictors are daily negative events and daily positive events. The hypothesis of interest concerns the strength of the relationship between self-esteem and positive events versus the strength of the relationship between self-esteem and negative events. Is the Bad stronger than the Good? The model is below:

Day level $\quad y_{ij} = \beta_{0j} + \beta_{1j}(\text{PosEvent}) + \beta_{2j}(\text{NegEvent}) + r_{ij}$

Person level $\quad \beta_{0j} = \gamma_{00} + u_{0j}$

$$\beta_{1j} = \gamma_{10} + u_{1j}$$

$$\beta_{2j} = \gamma_{20} + u_{2j}$$

As might be expected, the slope between self-esteem and positive events (γ_{10}) is positive – let us say .30 for this example – whereas the slope between self-esteem and negative events (γ_{20}) is negative – let us say −.35. Using contrast codes as in all the previous examples, these two coefficients would probably be significantly different from each other. An estimated difference would be .65 (1 * .30) + (−1 * −.35).

Nevertheless, it likely that the absolute values of the two coefficients are probably not different. The difference in absolute terms is very small. The absolute value (strength) of the positive events coefficient is .30, and the absolute value of the negative events coefficient is .35, a difference of only .05. The absolute values of these slopes can be compared by assigning each coefficient a weight of 1, recognizing that a constraint tests a weighted sum. In this case, the weighted sum would be −.05 (1 * .30 + 1 * −.35). If the coefficients were of meaningfully different magnitudes (e.g., +.30 and −.60), a constraint comparing the absolute sizes of the slopes might be significant because it would be .30 (1 * .30 + 1 * −.60).

By the way, in my research, the Bad tends to be stronger than the Good, at least in these types of analyses. For example, in Nezlek and Plesko (2001), we found that the within-person (day-level) relationship between self-concept clarity was stronger for negative events ($-.33$) than it was for positive events ($+.09$). Note that both coefficients were significant. The more negative events a person experienced in a day, the lower their self-concept clarity was. In contrast, the more positive events a person experienced in a day, the higher their self-concept clarity was. It was simply the case that negative events led to greater changes in self-concept clarity than positive events did.

No-intercept models

An important set of models in MLM for analyzing diary data are typically called no-intercept or zero-intercept models. In these models, the intercept is deleted, providing a basis to estimate directly coefficients representing specific values of members of categorical systems. Such categorical systems can be at any level of analysis. In combination with different coding options and comparisons of fixed effects (coefficients) as described previously, a virtually limitless variety of hypotheses can be tested with considerable specificity.

The key to understanding how such models work is to recognize the importance of generating predicted values to interpret results. For the moment, let us assume we have a social interaction diary study, with interactions nested within persons. By now, such terminology should be familiar. Interactions can be classified as dyads (only one other person is present) or non-dyads (more than one other person is present). For each interaction, two dummy codes are created: one represents if an interaction was a dyad (1 = dyad, 0 = non-dyad), and the other represents if an interaction was not a dyad (1 = non-dyad, 0 = dyad). Bear with me. Assume the outcome measure is satisfaction. At the interaction level, both dummy codes are entered uncentered and the intercept is dropped, as below:

Interaction level	$y_{ij} = \beta_{1j}(\text{Dyad}) + \beta_{2j}(\text{Non-dyad}) + r_{ij}$
Person level	$\beta_{1j} = \gamma_{10} + u_{1j}$
	$\beta_{2j} = \gamma_{20} + u_{2j}$

For dyadic interactions, Dyad $= 1$, and Non-dyad $= 0$, so the estimated satisfaction for dyadic interactions is $\beta_{1j} * 1 + \beta_{2j} * 0$ or, more simply, β_{1j}. For non-dyadic interactions, Dyad $= 0$ and Non-dyad $= 1$, so the estimated satisfaction for dyadic interactions is $\beta_{1j} * 0 + \beta_{2j} * 1$ or more simply, β_{2j}. Such a model provides a basis to compare the mean satisfaction in dyads versus the mean satisfaction in non-dyads by constraining the γ_{10} and γ_{20} to be equal.

You might be wondering now, why drop the intercept and use two dummy codes rather than keep the intercept and use only one code, as in the following?

Interaction level $\quad y_{ij} = \beta_{0j} + \beta_{1j}(\text{Dyad}) + r_{ij}$

Although such a model is perfectly valid and one might want to use it, it does not bring up to the person level estimates of the means for dyads and non-dyads. In this model, the intercept represents the expected outcome for non-dyads (i.e., when dyad = 0), and the slope represents the difference between dyads and non-dyads.

Returning to the two-dummy-coded model, variables can be added to the person-level models. This would provide a basis to compare relationships between a person-level variable and satisfaction in dyads to relationships between the same person-level variable and satisfaction in non-dyads. For example, social anxiety can be included in both person-level models as below:

Person level $\quad \beta_{1j} = \gamma_{10} + \gamma_{11}(\text{Social anxiety}) + u_{1j}$

$\quad\quad\quad\quad\quad\quad\ \beta_{2j} = \gamma_{20} + \gamma_{21}(\text{Social anxiety}) + u_{2j}$

By constraining the γ_{11} and γ_{21} coefficients to be equal, the strength of the relationship between social anxiety and satisfaction in dyads can be compared to the strength of the relationship between social anxiety and satisfaction in non-dyads. See Nezlek, Schaafsma, Safron, and Krejtz (in press) for an application of such models using a dummy code at level 1 representing whether participants (member of ethnic minorities) were interacting with in-group members or not.

The same type of analysis can be used at the trait level. Assume a daily diary study in which participants are from three ethnic groups, White, Black and Hispanic. Hypotheses of interest concern group differences in reactions to stress. The dependent measure is anxiety. The following model would estimate intercepts and slopes for the three groups. These estimates could then be compared using tests of fixed effects (constraints), as I have discussed previously. White, Black, and Hispanic are person-level dummy codes representing an individual's membership status in these groups. The level 2 coefficients representing the means for each ethnic group can be compared using tests of fixed effects.

Day level $\quad\quad\quad\ y_{ij} = \beta_{0j} + \beta_{1j}(\text{Stress}) + r_{ij}$

Person level $\quad\quad \beta_{0j} = \gamma_{10}(\text{White}) + \gamma_{20}(\text{Black}) + \gamma_{30}(\text{Hispanic}) + u_{0j}$

$\quad\quad\quad\quad\quad\quad\ \beta_{1j} = \gamma_{11}(\text{White}) + \gamma_{21}(\text{Black}) + \gamma_{31}(\text{Hispanic}) + u_{1j}$

Categorical coding schemes can be combined into a single system. Assume a daily diary study in which there are male and female participants who are either

Republicans or Democrats. The outcome measure is some type of daily measure about a political topic. Gender and party can be combined to create a four-category system, in which each category represents a unique combination of the two systems. With the following person-level model, one could compare any combination of the four categories, providing a basis to conduct the functional equivalent of a 2 × 2 ANOVA – an option that should please experimentalists among others.

$$\beta_{0j} = \gamma_{10}(\text{Fem-Dem}) + \gamma_{20}(\text{Fem-Rep}) + \gamma_{30}(\text{Male-Dem}) + \gamma_{30}(\text{Male-Rep}) + u_{0j}$$

Analyses that rely on a series of dummy-codes to represent categories have two important requirements. First, observations need to be able to be unambiguously placed into a single category. Only one dummy code in a set of dummy codes can have a value of 1. Second, if all the dummy codes are included in an analysis, the intercept must be dropped. Other than that, you can pretty much do what you want.

Standardizing measures

Unlike many other techniques, MLM analyses do not produce standardized estimates of coefficients. At present, it is simply not an option. This means that coefficients represent relationships in the metrics of the measures as they are entered into the analysis. It is possible, however, to estimate coefficients that are functionally standardized, or at the least, closer to it.

This is particularly straightforward at the person level. All one needs to do is to standardize person-level measures within the sample. The resulting coefficients will then be functionally standardized. The units in which person-level coefficients are denominated will be standard units, meaning that a 1 unit change in a coefficient will represent a change of 1 SD in that measure. Standardizing in this manner provides at least two advantages. First, it makes generating predicted values easier (i.e., 1 unit = 1 SD). Second, it stabilizes comparisons of coefficients involving person-level measures – see previous section on comparing coefficients. In this regard, it is important to note that standardizing person-level measures does not change the results of significance tests of individual coefficients. Such tests are "invariant under transformation."

The situation is not so straightforward at the diary level. One can standardize a diary-level measure across all diary-level observations. This can be done on what is called a "flat file," a file that does not take into account the nested structure of the data. For example, assume I have a daily diary study in which there are 1800 daily observations for 175 people. I can standardize a daily measure such as daily anxiety on this sample of 1800. The fact that there are 175 participants is irrelevant.

Such standardization *does not* produce standardized coefficients for diary-level relationships. All such a procedure does is set the total variance (diary + person) for a measure to 1.0. The ratio of diary-level and person-level variance may still vary across different measures. The primary purpose of such standardization is to reduce the influence that differences in the variances of diary-level measures may have on parameter estimates. In my experience, such standardization has not produced meaningful differences in the results of analyses. In part, this may be because the variances of my diary-level measures have not differed markedly.

Regardless, I do not recommend standardizing diary-level measures within a person. Depending upon the number of observations and the distribution of scores, the within-person variance for an individual may not be that reliable. Moreover, standardizing within persons eliminates person-level variances in the measures – everyone has a mean of 0. Such differences are an essential characteristic of the data.

What to report

In this section, I describe two of the technically focused aspects that I look for when reading and reviewing articles describing diary-style studies. We can assume that the literature has been reviewed, the hypotheses or expectations have been described, and so forth.

First, a description of the data collection protocol is needed. Exactly what were participants asked to do? This can include, but not be limited to, how often and how they were asked to provide diary-level data, the definitions of response scales, descriptions or definitions of options for categorical responses, and so forth. Of particular, absolutely critical, importance for event contingent studies is a description of how the target event was defined. Unless readers know exactly what was being studied, it will be impossible for them to judge the results and the conclusions.

Next, how well participants complied with the protocol needs to be described. This can probably be done at the end of the methods section. This can include a description of date and time stamps if the data were collected electronically, post-study interviews; basically, any information that can shed some light on whether people did what they were asked to do. As part of this, the criteria for deleting participants and diary-level entries need to be described, and the number of participants and entries that were deleted needs to be presented.

This should be done briefly. For example, in a daily diary study, it really does not matter if the data for 5 days were deleted because they were entered too early and 10 days of data were deleted because they were entered too late. It should suffice to describe the response window and to note that 15 days of data were not entered in the appropriate time window. Editors and reviewers may want to know more specific details, but readers (or at least this reader) probably do not.

After this, the final sample that was analyzed needs to be described. For the diary-level data, I recommend the following. For interval contingent studies, the average number of responses that were retained for analysis for each participant should be described, including some description of the variability such as the range and SD. You may also want to mention the percentage of participants who met some criterion. For example, 90% of participants provided at least 10 of 14 days of valid data, 88% of participants responded to at least 85% of requests for a response when beeped, and so forth. To impress readers, you may want to mention the total number of diary-level observations that were retained for analysis. For an event contingent study, you should describe the number of events per person (mean, SD, and range) and perhaps the total number of events. It is also probably best to describe the number of time periods (typically days) over which participants provided data. Once again, this should include the mean, SD, and range.

I have not discussed how to describe the participants themselves because you should be familiar with this already. You may want to describe differences (or typically, the lack thereof) between participants who were retained for analysis and those who were not. The importance of doing this will vary primarily as a function of the number of participants who were excluded – more participants, more important.

Now for the results. Although the utility of this will vary across studies and manuscripts, I think it is useful to provide some type of overview of the analytic strategy before the results per se are presented. If the data have been analyzed with some type of MLM, what was nested within what needs to be *explicitly* described, if not at the outset, at least somewhere. If another analytic strategy was used (e.g., measures of within-person variability per se), this should also be described. Even if there are some variations on the basic structure in later analyses, it will help readers enormously to have a general sense of how you analyzed the data.

Before the results of tests of hypotheses are presented, I recommend presenting summary statistics for both the person- and diary-level data. Once again, I will not discuss the person-level data – this should be familiar territory. For the diary-level data, assuming some type of MLM analyses, multilevel summary statistics should be presented. For two-level analyses, these data would be the mean, the diary-level variance, and the person-level variance. For three-level analyses (e.g., beeps within days within persons) these data would be the mean, beep-level variance, and the day- and person-level variances. These summary statistics can be obtained from unconditional analyses of the variables. Keep in mind that for categorical outcomes (e.g., yes/no items), which need to be analyzed with specific techniques (see section on non-linear outcomes), there is no level 1 variance estimate.

The order in which the results of analyses themselves should be presented can vary considerably across different studies. Although the logic of MLM is to build the level 1 model (diary level) first and then add predictors, this sequence may not provide the most coherent description of the results. Regardless, I think that at this point in time, authors should present the equations representing their models. Moreover, as I discussed before, I recommend following the Bryk and Raudenbush style. This is an equation for the diary (or occasion) level model accompanied by separate equations for each of the coefficients that are brought up to the next level(s) of analysis.

Such a presentation makes it much clearer to readers what has been modeled at each level of analysis. Although such equations may not be necessary for readers who are familiar with MLM analyses of diary data, not all readers will be familiar with diary data, MLM, or both. I specifically recommend the Bryk and Raudenbush approach, rather than presenting a single equation, because I think it highlights the level of analysis at which constructs have been measured. This may be particularly important when constructs at different levels of analysis have similar names. I ask you, which of the two presentations below (of a not-so-complicated analysis from a daily diary study) is easier to explain to someone, particularly someone who is not familiar with MLM?

Day level $\quad y_{ij} = \beta_{0j} + \beta_{1j}(\text{PosEvent}) + \beta_{2j}(\text{NegEvent}) + r_{ij}$

Person level $\quad \beta_{0j} = \gamma_{00} + \gamma_{01}(\text{SexCnt}) + \gamma_{02}(\text{CESD}) + u_{0j}$

$\qquad\qquad\quad \beta_{1j} = \gamma_{10} + \gamma_{11}(\text{SexCnt}) + \gamma_{12}(\text{CESD}) + u_{1j}$

$\qquad\qquad\quad \beta_{2j} = \gamma_{20} + \gamma_{21}(\text{SexCnt}) + \gamma_{22}(\text{CESD}) + u_{2j}$

Or you can present

$$y = \gamma_{00} + \gamma_{01} * \text{SexCnt} + \gamma_{02} * \text{CESD} + \gamma_{10} * \text{PosEvent} + \gamma_{11} * \text{SexCnt} * \text{PosEvent}$$
$$+ \gamma_{12} * \text{CESD} * \text{PosEvent} + \gamma_{20} * \text{NegEvent} + \gamma_{21} * \text{SexCnt} * \text{NegEvent}$$
$$+ \gamma_{22} * \text{CESD} * \text{NegEvent} + u_0 + u_1 * \text{PosEvent} + u_2 * \text{NegEvent} + r$$

I rest my case.

Regardless of how or if you depict your models in equation form, there is the issue of how to report and describe significance tests of coefficients. In this regard, for me, more is truly less. A full informed test of a fixed effect requires the coefficient itself, the t-ratio, and a p-level. The standard error (SE) does not need to be displayed, because t = coefficient/SE. You can present it if you want, but it is redundant. Also, I do not, pro forma, report the results of significance tests of error terms. If a zealous editor or reviewer wants them I will oblige, but rarely do hypotheses concern tests of error terms (see previous section on modeling error).

I also think it is helpful to provide a verbal description of what a coefficient actually represents. For example, if I had a coefficient (slope) of +.45 between daily stress and daily anxiety, I would write something such as: "This means that, on average, for every 1 unit (or 1 point) increase in daily stress, daily anxiety increased .45." The equation for the coefficient for negative events is below:

$$\beta_{1j} = \gamma_{10} + u_{1j}$$
$$\beta_{1j} = .45 + u_{1j}$$

Note two things about this explanation. First, it makes clear that this is an average coefficient or amount of change. The coefficient for some people may be larger or smaller than it is for others – possibilities that can be examined by looking at person-level moderators. Second, it makes clear that the measurement units are actual scores, not standardized scores. MLM analyses do not generate standard scores – see previous section on standardizing measures.

For cross-level interactions, e.g., when a diary-level relationship varies as a function of a person-level variable (a moderating relationship), I think it is critical to explain results by generating predicted values. To continue the previous example, assume that trait anxiety (standardized) moderated the within-person relationship between daily stress and daily anxiety, and the moderating coefficient was +.15. The equation and some hypothetical values are below:

$$\beta_{1j} = \gamma_{10} + \gamma_{11}(\text{Anxiety}) + u_{1j}$$
$$\beta_{1j} = .45 + .15(\text{Anxiety}) + u_{1j}$$

Traditionally, results from regression-style analyses are illustrated by computing predicted scores for observations that are ±1 SD on the predictors. If trait anxiety had been standardized before analysis, it would have been quite straightforward to generate coefficients for participants who were ±1 SD on trait anxiety. The mean coefficient was .45, so a person who was −1 SD on trait anxiety would have an expected coefficient of .30 (.45 − 1 * .15). For a person who was +1 SD on trait anxiety, the expected coefficient would be .60 (.45 + 1 * .15). This is exactly the type of information I recommend including in a manuscript. Even readers who are not familiar with MLM will be able to understand a within-person relationship.

If trait anxiety had not been standardized, the moderating coefficient would be different than if it had been standardized. Nevertheless, the same procedure would be followed to estimate predicted values, and the predicted values would be the same. If the SD for trait anxiety had been 2, the moderating coefficient would have been .075.

I do not recommend reporting the results of tests of sequential models. Such tests include both the fixed and random effects (including the covariances of the random effects), whereas most hypotheses concern only the fixed effects. There may be some instances when such tests serve a purpose (West et al., 2011), but, generally, the information they provide does not bear on research hypotheses per se.

Effect sizes

Traditionally, i.e., for OLS analyses, effect sizes are commonly estimated by comparing error variances of different models, and effect sizes are typically measured in terms of the percentage that such error variances are reduced from one model to the next. Although this technique can be applied to estimating effect sizes within the multilevel context (and I provide some examples below), I urge analysts to be cautious as they do so. In this regard, I suspect that I have a somewhat more conservative position about effect sizes than some multilevel modelers and practitioners. Regardless, I recommend heeding the advice of Kreft and de Leeuw, two well-respected multilevel modelers, who wrote: "In general, we suggest not setting too much store by the calculation of R_B^2 [level-2 variance] or R_W^2 [level-1 variance]" (1998: 119). These are the residual variances that some use to estimate effect sizes.

My conservatism reflects the fact that residual variance estimates in MLM are not the same as error variances in OLS analyses. As discussed previously, in MLM analyses, each coefficient can have two variance estimates, one for the fixed effect and one for the random effect, and the variance of the random effect is typically considered as the error term for purposes of estimating effect sizes. Moreover, as estimates based on covariance matrices, the estimate of the random variance for a specific coefficient can change as a function of including or deleting predictors for other coefficients. It is all one, big, happy family.

More problematic is the possibility that adding *significant* predictors to a model may not reduce the error variance. In OLS, significance tests for predictors are predicated on reductions in variance – no reduction in variance, no significance. In contrast, in MLM, the variance of the fixed effects (the standard errors that are used to conduct significance tests) and the variance of the random effects (used to estimate effect sizes à la OLS) are estimated separately. In MLM, the significance test of a predictor is not predicated on a reduction in variance. This is the nature of the maximum likelihood algorithms used in MLM analyses. I will note that, in my experience, adding significant predictors that did not lead to a reduction in error variances has been more common at level 1 (the diary level) than at level 2 (the person level).

Other issues arise, however, in evaluating effect sizes in the analysis of coefficients brought up to the person level. Assume a simple day-level model as below. Predictors could be added to the person-level equations.

Day level $\quad y_{ij} = \beta_{0j} + \beta_{1j}(\text{PosEvent}) + \beta_{2j}(\text{NegEvent}) + r_{ij}$

Person level $\quad \beta_{0j} = \gamma_{00} + u_{0j}$

$$\beta_{1j} = \gamma_{10} + u_{1j}$$

$$\beta_{2j} = \gamma_{20} + u_{2j}$$

First, the day-level predictors need to be entered group-mean centered. If they are not, then the variances of the predictors across the two levels of the analysis are not separated, meaning that reductions in variance at any one level will include variance from both levels. Second, to estimate effect sizes for a moderating analysis of a slope (the γ_{10} and γ_{20} coefficients for positive and negative events in this example), the coefficient needs to be modeled as randomly varying, i.e., the error term needs to be included. If the random variance is not estimated, then it is not possible to calculate a change in the random variance. Also, recall from the previous section on modeling error that individual differences in coefficients can be examined even if a random error term is not estimated for a coefficient. Such coefficients are called non-randomly varying.

Keeping these caveats in mind, estimating effect sizes in MLM follows the same logic as estimating effect sizes in OLS. Assume the day-level random variance in the above example was .66, and when the two event scores were included, this was reduced to .45. The reduction in variance expressed as a percentage would be 32% (.21/.66), corresponding to a multiple R of .56. By the way, I know of no way to estimate the variance of one predictor while controlling for the other predictor, similar to partial or semi-partial correlations in OLS regression.

As I said previously, I urge analysts to be cautious when presenting effect sizes within the MLM framework. In my experience, there seem to be few problems estimating effect sizes when a single predictor is included – the issue of adding significant predictors that do not reduce error is moot. Nevertheless, I do not think the procedure is as straightforward and trouble-free as many authors seem to believe, and when I include estimates of effect sizes (often at the insistence of a reviewer or editor), I include a brief description of the possible limitations of such estimates.

Non-linear outcomes and analyses of relative quantity of events

The vast majority of diary studies concern continuous outcomes that are assumed to be, more or less, normally distributed. Nevertheless, some outcomes are not continuous or normally distributed. For example, in social interaction diary study, analyses of the percentage of interactions of a certain type (e.g., with a romantic partner) rely upon dichotomous measures (e.g., 1 = partner present, 0 = not present), which by definition are not normally distributed. In a daily diary study, whether a certain type of event occurred each day (e.g., an argument) can also be represented by a dichotomous measure. Various other diary-level measures may also not be normally distributed. These include categorical outcomes (ordered or not) and count data; for example, an outcome occurs only once on most days, twice on fewer days, three times on fewer days than twice, and so forth. A good example of an application of this technique can be found in O'Grady, Cullum, Armeli, and Tennen (2011), a diary study of alcohol consumption. Note that this list of non-linear outcomes is not meant to be exhaustive, just illustrative.

An important feature of non-linear outcomes is that they cannot be analyzed using the same algorithms as linear outcomes because they violate too many assumptions. For example, for binary outcomes, the mean and the variance are not independent (the variance = $\sqrt{(npq)}$, where n = number of observations, p = proba-bility of the outcome, and $q = 1 - p$), and such independence is a very important assumption. For OLS regression, such outcomes are typically analyzed using logis-tical regression.

There are multilevel equivalents of logistical regression, and when you have a non-linear outcome, you need to use these techniques. The logic of conducting a multilevel logistical analysis is the same as the logic of conducting multilevel analyses of linear measures – you estimate a level 1 model, add predictors, and so forth. The critical difference between analyzing non-linear and linear outcomes is that, for non-linear outcomes, the level 1 data are transformed so that they no longer violate critical assumptions. The specific transformation that is required varies as a function of the nature of the outcome, and I cannot describe all of these transformations here. I will illustrate the techniques by describing the analysis of a dichotomous measure (0, 1).

Assume a social interaction diary study and the hypotheses of interest con-cern the percentage of interactions involving a romantic partner. Interactions are nested within persons, and the outcome measure is coded 1 if a romantic partner is present and 0 if one is not – sometimes called a Bernoulli outcome. The level 1 and 2 models (with the transformation for a Bernoulli outcome at level 1) is below:

$$\text{Prob}(y = 1|\beta_{0j}) = \phi$$

$$\beta_{0j} = \gamma_{00} + u_{1j}$$

Similar to the analysis of linear outcomes, in this model, a coefficient, ϕ, is esti-mated for each level 2 unit. This coefficient is sometimes referred to as a "logit." Keep in mind that for a Bernoulli model such as this, the null hypothesis is that 50% of interactions are with a romantic partner. The mean logit (γ_{00}) is 0. If there were more categories, the null would be that the percentage of interactions in each category is the same (e.g., 33% in each category if there were three). Note that there is no level 1 variance estimate in such analyses.

Similar to the analysis of continuous measures, these logits are then analyzed at level 2. Moreover, predictors can be added at all levels of analysis. For example, the following person-level model would examine the relationship between percentage of interactions with a romantic partner and a person-level measure of attachment:

$$\beta_{0j} = \gamma_{00} + \gamma_{01}(\text{Attachment}) + u_{0j}$$

The results of such analyses can be interpreted in various ways. One straightforward way is to estimate the percentage of interactions based upon the estimated coefficients. For those who are inexperienced with such models, this can involve some complicated calculations, which I have always done using a spreadsheet such as Excel. Another way of interpreting such analyses (popular in some other disciplines in which logistical regression is more common) is to calculate "odd ratios" – see Nezlek (2011) for a discussion. In Nezlek (2011) I also discuss different ways of analyzing outcomes that have more than two response categories.

Multilevel logistical regression is a topic with its own following, and I cannot do it justice in this volume. Nevertheless, to me, one of its most useful applications for diary researchers is to examine the distribution of diary-level observations, e.g., the percentage of days on which an argument occurred, the percentage of interactions of a certain type, and so forth. Distinguishing the *relative* quantity (frequency) of an event versus the absolute quantity is needed when the baseline number of events varies across persons. For example, the number of social interactions people have varies widely. If one were to analyze the number of interactions a person had per day with a romantic partner, individual differences in how socially active people were per se would be part of this analysis.

Assume that, on average, Person A has eight interactions per day and that two of these involve his romantic partner. In contrast, Person B has three interactions per day and one of these involves her romantic partner. Analyses of the *absolute* quantity of contact (discussed in a section below) would find that Person A had more contact with his romantic partner (two per day) than Person B had with hers (one per day). In contrast, analyses of the *relative* quantity of contact would find that Person A had less contact with his romantic partner (25%) than Person B had with hers (33%). Neither of these measures is correct per se. The selection of which to use will depend upon the questions of interest at hand.

Data problems

When designing experiments, researchers typically have a good idea of how the data will be analyzed. For example, factorial designs will require some type of ANOVA, perhaps an ANCOVA, with the possible addition of some type of mediational analysis. Regardless, experimentalists can be relatively certain that the data they need to conduct the analyses they want to conduct will be available to them. By definition, experimentalists control the conditions under which data are collected, and unless they object, participants provide the data that are needed to conduct the analyses that the researcher wants to conduct. Certainly, additional or unanticipated analyses of data collected within an experimental context are conducted, but by and large the analyses go according to plan. Not the results perhaps, but the structure of the analyses themselves is largely predetermined.

In contrast, there is more uncertainty about the data collected in a diary study. It is entirely possible that the data that are collected will not provide the basis for conducting the analyses that were envisioned when the study was designed. For example, a researcher may be interested in comparing the within-person relationships between mood and two types of stressors. If participants do not experience both of these stressors with sufficient frequency during a study to provide a basis for analysis, then such a comparison will not be possible. Similarly, a researcher may be interested in comparing interactions with opposite-sex, non-romantic friends to interactions with opposite-sex romantic partners. If participants do not have many (or any) interactions with such friends, such comparisons cannot be made – full stop. A great strength of diary-style studies is that they describe "life as it is lived" (Bolger et al., 2003). Well, if life as people live it does not fit neatly into the pigeonholes that researchers need to fill to make the comparisons they think are important, then researchers need to adjust their pigeonholes and analyses accordingly.

How to accommodate your analytic strategy to the realities of your data will vary considerably as a function of the specific data you have and the questions at hand. An important guiding principle is to ensure that whatever measures you analyze occur with a sufficient frequency to provide a basis to estimate parameters. For example, in a social interaction diary study, individuals may report interacting with many different types of family members but only once or twice with each type. Although it might be theoretically desirable to distinguish aunts and uncles, grandmothers and grandfathers, and the like, if there are not enough interactions with each of these types of relatives, it will not be possible to make such distinctions. In such a case, you might create a variable "family member" that includes aunts, uncles, grandparents, and so forth.

6

Multilevel analyses of diary data: Some applications and advanced topics

Nesting and number of levels of analysis

Typically, the basic structure of the data generated by a diary study is reasonably obvious. In a daily diary study, days are nested within persons; in a social interaction diary study, interactions are nested within persons; and so forth. Nevertheless, there are occasions when such basic structures are questioned. For example, in a "beeper study" should occasions be nested within days, which are then nested within persons? What is gained by adding an extra level, or, perhaps more important, what might be lost or confounded by not doing so? In this section, I discuss some of the factors that need to be taken into account when making such decisions. In some situations, I think what needs to be done is reasonably clear, whereas in others it is not. I provide recommendations when I think they are warranted, and I withhold them when I think the situation is ambiguous.

When conceptualizing the basic structure of the analyses of a set of diary data, I think one needs to start with an understanding of what a level of analysis means conceptually. As discussed in the section on the logic of MLM, it is useful to think of the levels of an analysis as representing different samples. A consequence of this is that if there are not enough units of analysis to constitute a sample, it may not be wise to add a level of analysis that models the variability associated with sampling these units.

For example, in a study described in Nezlek et al. (2008b), we collected daily diary data in four different places: Canada, Japan, and two sites in the USA. Initially, we conceptualized the analyses as three-level models, days within persons, and persons within sites. Although it was possible to set up such models, they did not run well. For example, we could not estimate the random variability for all sorts of terms that, based on previous research, we should have been able to model as random. There were lots of convergence problems and so forth. In brief, we simply did not have enough data to estimate the parameters of such three-level models.

The solution was to move site "down" to the person level. That is, site became a person-level variable. This was done with a series of dummy codes with no intercepts in the person-level model. The models performed very well. We had no problems estimating random error terms, models converged quickly, and so forth. The essential limitation of this procedure is that site became a fixed effect. Our inference was limited only to the four sites where we had collected data. If we had had 20 sites, we probably would have had enough to draw inferences about the population of sites (actually cultures in our case); however, we did not, and no amount of tinkering with the model could make this happen.

The structure of the final models is presented below. Assume a dependent measure of anxiety with daily stress as a predictor. The US1, US2, CA, and JP variables are dummy codes, each representing one of the four sites. They were entered uncentered, and the intercepts for the person-level equations were dropped. Differences between sites were tested by constraining coefficients to be equal.

Day level $\qquad y_{ij} = \beta_{0j} + \beta_{1j}(\text{Stress}) + r_{ij}$

Person level $\quad \beta_{0j} = \gamma_{01}(\text{US1}) + \gamma_{02}(\text{US2}) + \gamma_{03}(\text{CA}) + \gamma_{04}(\text{JP}) + u_{0j}$

$\qquad\qquad\quad \beta_{1j} = \gamma_{11}(\text{US1}) + \gamma_{12}(\text{US2}) + \gamma_{13}(\text{CA}) + \gamma_{14}(\text{JP}) + u_{1j}$

In this particular case, it made sense to compare the four sites. They were meaningfully different in ways that we thought would be relevant to the issues at hand. There may be situations, however, when participants can be classified in terms of group membership, but it may not be meaningful to distinguish the groups. For example, if a study involved students from four different introductory psychology classes, it would be difficult to think that there would be much interest in comparing them, unless of course they differed in some systematic way. In contrast, if a study involved students from two psychology classes and two economics classes, it might be meaningful to compare them.

In some cases, the lack of a sufficient number of units of observations may reflect the nature of the population itself. For example, in a diary study, there is no need to nest observations within persons and then nest persons within sex. There are only two sexes, or at the least, for most intents and purposes, there are two. Sex differences can be tested using either contrast or dummy codes as described in the previous section on coding.

The same considerations come into play when conceptualizing the diary-level data. For example, in a daily diary study, participants may provide data on weekends and weekdays. One way to think of such data would be to think of nesting days within type of day (weekday vs. weekend) and type of day within persons. Aside from the fact that there are only two types of days (not enough for a sample, as just discussed), there is also the fact that there is no population of types of days to which one can make an inference. There are only two types of days, not a large sample of days such as the sample of countries as described in the above example.

In such cases, type of day becomes a fixed effect and is represented as a day-level variable. The logic for this is similar to that used for the previous example, and as discussed in the section on coding, this can be done in two ways. Similar to the models just described, type of day could be represented by two dummy coded variables at the day level, one for weekdays (1 = weekday, 0 = weekend) and another for weekends (0 = weekday, 1 = weekend). Each day would be coded on both variables, and they would both be entered uncentered and the intercept would be dropped.

Day level $\quad y_{ij} = \beta_{1j}(\text{WDAY}) + \beta_{2j}(\text{WEND}) + r_{ij}$

As shown below, this would bring "up" to the person level estimated means for the outcome measure separately for weekends and weekdays. These means could be compared using constraints on the model. Person-level predictors can be added to this basic model to examine relationships between traits and daily experience on weekdays vs. weekends, and these coefficients can be compared:

Person level $\quad \beta_{1j} = \gamma_{10} + \gamma_{11}(\text{Trait}) + u_{1j}$

$\qquad\qquad\quad \beta_{2j} = \gamma_{20} + \gamma_{21}(\text{Trait}) + u_{2j}$

Another way to represent type of days would be with a contrast variable (DayCnt, weekday = 1, weekend = −1). Such an analysis estimates a difference score between weekend and weekdays, which is then brought up to the person level. Note that the intercept is retained in this model. The meaning of the intercept will vary as a function of how DayCnt is centered – see previous section on centering.

Day level $\quad y_{ij} = \beta_{0j} + \beta_{1j}(\text{DayCnt}) + r_{ij}$

In other cases, although an additional level of nesting at the within-person level may seem warranted, it may not be possible to include this level and it may not be appropriate to represent it with some type of fixed effect. For example, if participants provided 12 responses a day for two days (a beeper study), this could be thought of as a three-level design: occasions (beeps) nested within days and days nested within persons. As just discussed, however, two days does not provide an adequate basis to estimate the variance associated with sampling days, and so a three-level model is not appropriate.

This begs the question, "Why not nest beeps within persons and represent day at the beep level with some type of contrast or dummy code?" Although this is technically possible, it is not clear that this would be good practice. It is difficult to imagine that there would be any interest in differences between the first and second days per se. As is the case in most diary studies, they are probably just two days, not distinguishable in any meaningful way. If they were meaningfully different (as in weekends vs. weekdays) then it would make sense to add some type of code to compare them. If this were not the case, it would make the most sense to nest beeps within persons and be done with it. Yes, this would introduce day-level variability into the beep-level relationships, but there are not enough days to estimate the day-level variability.

Now for the most vexing issue – assuming you got through all that. How many units does it take to constitute a level of analysis? To me, this is an unusually difficult question to answer. Certainly, two are too few, and twenty are enough. That is the easy part. What about eight or ten? Given the absence (to my knowledge) of a theoretically or empirically based answer to such a question, I can offer only an opinion informed by my experience.

Similar to the considerations raised in the section on power and sample size, one of the issues is how reliable the within-unit coefficients are. More reliable coefficients require fewer observations (units) to model than less reliable coefficients require. For example, it is entirely possible to have a beeper study that lasts 10 days and that provides the data to estimate the day-level variability within the context of a three-level model: occasion within days within persons. It is also possible that 10 days will not provide enough data. At present, the only way to determine this is to run analyses with the "additional" level of analysis included and see what happens. If the data do not provide the basis for estimating the random variance for terms that you know should be random (e.g., slopes), you have exceeded the "carrying capacity" of the data.

My experience is that if the within-unit coefficients are reliable, then 10+ units can provide an adequate (although not desirable or optimal) basis for estimating the unit-level variance in coefficients. Keep in mind that means (intercepts) are invariably more reliable than slopes, and so the same design might be able to estimate the variance associated with intercepts but not for slopes. Also, as more and more coefficients are being estimated at a level of analysis, the data may be stretched. For example, if a within-day model has three predictors, 10 days may not be enough to estimate the between-day variance in all the within-day coefficients (and the covariances among the error terms), whereas the same data set might be able to estimate a within-day model with only one predictor.

To me, the nether-world is between five and ten units. With five or fewer units, I feel comfortable either ignoring a level of analysis or representing the units with some type of code at another level of analysis. For example, I would not nest beeps nested within days in a beeper study with five or fewer days, and I would not nest persons within groups with five or fewer groups. If there are more than five days in a beeper study, I would begin to think about adding the day as a level, but in most cases I probably would not be able to. There would simply not be enough data. Similarly, any number of groups can be represented with a series of codes, but as the number of groups increases, this can become unwieldy. If I had eight groups, I might try a three level model, but my guess is that the final analysis would either ignore the groups or represent them with a series of codes at the person level.

What risks does one take by ignoring or not taking into account a level of analysis? The primary risk is that when a level of analysis is not taken into account, the variance at the level of analysis is combined (and confounded) with the variance at another level of analysis. By the way, as discussed initially, separating variances at different levels of analysis is the raison d'être for doing MLM in the first place.

For example, assume a beeper study conducted over two days with five occasions each day, measuring two variables, X and Y. The hypothetical data for one participant are presented below. Within each of the two days, the relationship between X and Y is negative. In contrast, the relationship between X and Y is positive if the 10 observations are analyzed together, i.e., if nesting occasions within days are ignored. I will allow you to use your imagination to consider how ignoring nesting in other ways might lead to similar problems.

Day	Occasion	X	Y
1	1	1	4
1	2	2	2
1	3	2	2
1	4	3	1
1	5	1	4
2	1	4	8
2	2	6	6
2	3	6	6
2	4	7	5
2	5	5	8

As I have been discussing, without a sufficient number of observations one cannot incorporate all the levels of nesting that one might want to take into account. Analysts are limited to analyzing the data that have been collected. Nevertheless, a knowledge of such issues may help researchers conceptualize and design studies so that sufficient data are available to estimate parameters of interest and avoid confounding levels of analysis.

Analyzing quantity in event contingent studies including size of social network

Although multilevel analyses of interval and event contingent data are structurally similar in many ways, there is an important, substantive difference between the two types of studies regarding what I will refer to as "quantity." In interval contingent studies, the number of records a person provides (number of days, number of momentary reports, etc.) is typically of little interest, aside perhaps from serving as a basis to exclude participants who have not complied with a data collection protocol. Moreover, although it is possible to classify records (e.g., days) as possessing a characteristic or not (e.g., did an argument occur?), most diary-style research focuses on continuous outcomes (e.g., West et al., 2011). Nevertheless, if hypotheses of interest concern the relative frequency of an outcome (e.g., the percentage of observations that fall into a certain category), the frequency of occurrence of that outcome can be modeled as a binary outcome using the techniques described in the previous section on non-linear outcomes.

In contrast, in an event contingent study, the number of events individuals record may constitute meaningful data. For example, in a study of social interaction, the number of interactions a person has is meaningful, the amount of time a person spends per day in interaction is meaningful, the number of different people with whom an individual interacts is meaningful, and so forth. Moreover, it seems that, at least in the case of social interaction, the reactions people have to their social interactions (quality) are distinct from how socially active they are (Nezlek, 2000). For example, in both collegiate (Nezlek, Imbrie, & Shean, 1994) and community samples (Nezlek, Hampton, & Shean, 2000), depressive symptoms have been found to be negatively related to the quality of interaction (satisfaction, closeness to others, control). In contrast, in these studies, depressive symptoms were not significantly related to the amount and distribution of interaction.

Many published studies that use social interaction diaries do not report the results of analyses of interaction quantity. I am not certain if this is because no interesting or meaningful results were found, or because the analyses were not conducted. Moreover I do not know that the importance of distinguishing quality and quantity of events has been demonstrated for events other than social interactions. Nevertheless, if measures of the quantity of an event are not analyzed, we are "left hanging" in terms of fully understanding the event being studied.

For social interactions, one straightforward way to study quantity of interaction is to tally the number of events people have each day and do a MLM in which days are nested within persons and the outcome is number of interactions. A related alternative is to create a measure of how much time people spend in interaction. Most interaction diary studies ask people how long their interactions are, and so such measures are typically easy to create. More subtle distinctions can be made for number of interactions and time spent in interaction by creating tallies for different types of interactions. For example, a researcher might be interested in time spent with close friends or romantic partners.

Such measures are relatively easy to create in most data analysis packages. For example, assume a social interaction diary study in which participants are identified by the variable ID, the day an interaction occurred is represented by the variable JDATE, the length of an interaction is represented by the variable LENGTH. If the interaction-level data are sorted by ID and within ID by JDATE, in SPSS the following commands will create day-level measures that contain the number of interactions (NUMPD) and the amount of time spent in interaction

(TIMEPD). These records are read into a file named "day_data." These commands can be generated by clicking on "Data" then "Aggregate" and then follow the dialog boxes from there. (Hints: ID and JDATE are the "break" variables and proper sorting is critical.)

```
AGGREGATE
/OUTFILE='day_data'
/PRESORTED
/BREAK=ID,JDATE
/TIMEPD=sum(LENGTH)
/NUMPD=N.
```

Interactions meeting certain criteria can be selected in advance of such aggregation to create measures representing certain types of interactions (e.g., interactions with close others). Keep in mind that such procedures require some type of representation in each interaction record of whether an interaction is of a certain type or not. These day-level data can then be nested within participants and analyzed. Depending upon the distribution of interactions, the outcome may need to be treated as non-linear (see previous section), but the data structure and resulting analytic strategies are fairly clear.

One important question that arises when conducting such analyses is how to treat days on which no interactions were described. For analyses of quality, in which interactions are nested within persons (even when interactions are nested within days within persons), the question is moot. If there are no interactions recorded for a day, that day is not included in the analysis.

Historically, my colleagues and I have assumed that days on which no interactions were recorded were days that participants skipped. Given that the participants in most of these studies were collegians, we felt comfortable assuming this. Most university settings provide ample and convenient access to peers, and most important, in post-study interviews, when a day was missing, participants invariably said that they forgot to record their interactions of that day.

Nevertheless, I recommend that researchers who are interested in studying the quantity of an event explicitly determine why no events are described for particular days. Given the commonplace nature of social interaction, it may be safe to assume that most people interact with someone each day, and so even for non-collegians, days with no interactions may be rare. This may not be the case, however, for other types of events such as sexual interactions, arguments, and business meetings. Determining why no events were recorded on certain days can be relatively easy to do – just ask participants. If an event did not occur on a day, a value of 0 can be entered.

Although the previous discussion has explained the analyses of quantity of events within the context of social interaction diary studies, the techniques I have described can be straightforwardly applied to event contingent studies in which some other type of event triggers the generation of a record. The time period that is used to organize the count may vary. For example, for some types of events, it might make sense to use a week as an organizing unit. Making such decisions will depend upon the topic and the nature of the questions at hand.

There is one characteristic of social interaction that requires slightly different treatment, however – the analysis of the number of different people with whom someone interacted. This can be understood in one of two ways: the number of different people with whom someone interacted each day (or some other organizing unit); and the number of different people with whom some interacted during a study per se. The second could be considered a measure of the size of social networks – depending upon how one defines such a network.

Essential to such analyses are descriptions of the specific people with whom participants interacted during the study. In most diary studies, I have asked participants to record up to three different people who were present, and interactions with three or fewer others account for about 85% of interactions. For larger interactions, you may decide to ask people to describe the people with whom they spent the most time during the interaction. See Appendix 1: Sample social interaction diary instructions for examples of such instructions.

Assuming these data are available (you cannot analyze social networks if they are not), the first step is to create a file that contains only the participant code (ID) and the initials of the different people with whom the participant interacted (represented as INIT1, INIT2, INIT3). The code below will do this in SPSS. (Hint: If you are using the point and click dialog boxes, you will need to click on the box "Number of cases." If you want to, you can rename the count variable (N_BREAK) when doing this.)

The input file is an interaction-level data set, one record for each interaction (as discussed above). It is best if the file is sorted by participant ID and within ID by day and then within day by starting time of the interaction. Thus, a place for everything and everything in its place.

The logic is as follows. First, a file is created that generates a record for each combination of participant and initials. Second, a file is created that contains the number of times that each set of initials in each participant's record appeared. Third, a file is created that contains the number of unique sets of initials that appeared in each participant's record. This last file will have one line of data for each participant.

1   Create a new file with a variable "Initial." Each record in the file will have the initials from each interaction, one record for each initial. For interactions that were with only one other person, only one record will be written (one set of initials); if two others were present, two records will be written; and so forth. The last command "NULL=DROP" signals the program not to write a record if the initial field is missing (blank). If the command is "NULL=KEEP" then every interaction will produce three records.

```
VARSTOCASES
/MAKE Initial FROM INIT1 INIT2 INIT3
/INDEX=Index1(3)
/KEEP=ID
/NULL=DROP.
```

2   Next, you sort this file by ID and then within ID by Initial. Then you count the number of times each initial appears. This may not be of interest per se, but it is an intermediate step to calculating the number of different initials in the entire diary. It goes to the file "initial_temp."

```
AGGREGATE
/OUTFILE='initial_temp'
/PRESORTED
/BREAK=ID Initial
/N_BREAK=N.
```

3   Finally, you count the number of different initials in each participant's record, and this total is written to file "initial_final." You should have a file that has the same number of records as you have participants. To control for the possibility that participants maintained their diaries for different numbers of days, this final value should be divided by the number of days a participant maintained a diary. Integrate the number of days from another file if need be. See previous section on data preparation.

```
DATASET ACTIVATE initial_temp.
AGGREGATE
/OUTFILE='initial_final'
/PRESORTED
/BREAK=ID
/N_BREAK=N.
```

Just in case that was not enough for you, it is also possible to calculate the number of different initials that appear each day. This file can be treated as a day-level file. As was the case with the number of interactions per day, you may need to model the outcome measure as non-linear, but the nesting is days within persons. I present the SPSS code without explanation, other than to note that the critical difference between these commands and the previous set of commands is the addition of the day (JDATE), as an organizing level of aggregation. The resulting file allows for nice analyses of the number of different people with whom someone interacts in a day.

```
VARSTOCASES
/MAKE Initial FROM INIT1 INIT2 INIT3
/INDEX=Index1(3)
/KEEP=ID,JDATE
/NULL=DROP.
```

```
AGGREGATE
/OUTFILE='initialday_temp'
/PRESORTED
/BREAK=ID JDATE Initial

/N_BREAK=N.
DATASET ACTIVATE initialday_temp.
AGGREGATE
/OUTFILE='initialday_final'
/PRESORTED
/BREAK=ID JDATE
/N_BREAK=N.
```

I realize that, for some, these analyses may be a "bit over the top." That is, why bother? Although I can appreciate such a reaction, my sense is that researchers have not studied quantity of social contact per se because a template or organizing structure for such analyses was not readily available. One of my goals in writing this book was to provide such templates, and I hope this section achieves that goal.

Evaluating the reliability and validity of diary-level measures

Regardless of how carefully items have been chosen, researchers may need to address concerns about the reliability and validity of the measures that they use at the diary level. When evaluating reliability and validity, I think of evaluating reliability as more of a science, whereas I think of evaluating validity as more of an art. That is, the procedures used to measure reliability produce definitive estimates or values, which can be accepted as reliable or not. In contrast, the procedures used to evaluate validity are somewhat more subjective. Validity is typically evaluated in terms of the correspondence between scores on a measure and scores on some other measure or criterion, and there may be legitimate differences of opinion about what constitutes appropriate criterion measures.

Nevertheless, for most diary-style studies, the primary concern is for the item level reliability of measures that have been administered on a repeated basis. For example, do the four items measuring self-esteem that have been administered each day or for each interaction measure the same construct? (I address the issue of validity later.) This is functionally equivalent to determining Cronbach's alpha for more traditional single assessment measures. When evaluating the item-level reliability of a set of items within the context of a diary study, it is critical to take into account the nested structure of the data. Before discussing how item-level reliability should be estimated, I discuss some common ways that item-level reliabilities have been estimated incorrectly, with apologies to all involved.

1 Calculate within-person means for the items making up a scale and then use these
   means as the basis for a person-level analysis to estimate Cronbach's alpha.

Problems: Such analyses are fundamentally flawed because they rely upon
between-person covariances to estimate a within-person phenomenon. As discussed earlier, between- and within-person relationships are mathematically independent. Any relationship between two measures can exist at one level of analysis
while a completely different relationship exists at another level of analysis.
Cronbach's alpha is based upon the covariances among the scores for individuals,
and so Cronbach's alpha based on means aggregated within individuals is based
upon between-person covariances. Each person has one score on each item (their
mean response on that item). The resulting alpha reflects relationships at the
between-person level, whereas the question concerns relationships at the
within-person (diary) level. Although estimates of reliability based upon aggregates may tell us something, they do not tell us anything about how consistently
participants respond to a set of items on each measurement occasion.

2 Organize the data (somehow) in terms of the days in a diary, calculate an alpha for
   each day, and then average these alphas.

Problems: Such analyses are typically fundamentally flawed because they assume
that days (occasions of measurement) are fixed rather than random. Typically,
there is no basis to assume that day 1 (or any day for that matter) for person 1
corresponds to day 1 for person 2, day 1 for person 3, and so forth. In a diary
study, the days on which participants provide data typically have no particular
meaning – they are sampled from the population of days, and, as such, occasions
of measurement need to be treated as a random effect. Moreover, it is not clear
how such a technique would be applied when participants have different numbers
of days or start on different days. Should the organizing theme be specific calen-
dar days (put all the data for June 5 together, for June 6, etc.), the sequence of the
day in a participant's diary (first, second, third, etc.), or the sequence of the day
participants were meant to provide data? Similarly, it is not clear how such a
technique could be applied when occasions of measurement are explicitly meant
to differ across individuals as is the case with the random sampling in most beeper
studies. Finally, such an approach is, on its face, utterly inappropriate for event
contingent data structures such as those that are created by social interaction diary
studies. There is no rationale for grouping interactions described by one participant with those described by another.
    In terms of this issue, I urge analysts to be cautious using various techniques that
have been proposed to estimate reliability within the context of repeated measures
designs or diary studies. For example, Cranford and colleagues (e.g., Cranford et al.,
2006) proposed an approach based upon generalizability theory to estimate the reliability of measures of daily mood in diary studies. Although technically accurate,

their analyses assumed that the days the diaries their participants maintained were fixed. Day 1 for participant 1 was matched with day 1 for participant 2, which was matched with day 1 for participant 3, and so forth. Although this assumption may have been tenable for the specific data sets with which they dealt, as discussed previously it is an untenable assumption for most diary studies, and it is entirely inappropriate for event contingent data.

I also urge analysts to be cautious when using methods based upon SEM analyses of longitudinal data to estimate reliability for measures collected at the diary level. Once again, such analyses assume that occasions of measurement are fixed. In longitudinal studies, measures are taken at fixed intervals (e.g., every six months for a few years). In such instances, it is sensible and proper to group observations as a function of the age of the participant, irrespective of the actual absolute date on which data are collected. All measurements taken when individuals are 25 years and 6 months old can be grouped, just as all measurements taken when individuals are 26 years and 6 months old can be grouped.

I recommend the following procedure to examine the reliability of a set of items that have been administered at the diary level. The general strategy is to conduct an analysis in which items are nested within occasions and occasions are nested within people. This procedure has the advantages of simplicity and broad application. It is easy to implement, and it can be used for different types of diary data. The technique can be used with any type of interval or event contingent method. There are no assumptions or restrictions on the spacing between observations, the number of observations per person, and so forth.

The procedure is based on the fact that (as discussed above) MLM programs (e.g., HLM) can provide estimates of the reliability of coefficients. Keep in mind that within the multilevel framework, reliability refers to the ratio of true to total variance (the classic definition of the reliability of a scale). When items are nested within occasions, the reliability of the level 1 intercept represents the ratio of true to total variance of the items, or the reliability of the items considered as observed measures of the same latent construct. Note that this reliability estimate is controlled for occasion and person-level differences in means.

The following data sets illustrate how to set up such analyses. The example consists of a social interaction diary study in which interactions are treated as nested within persons. A more complete and detailed example of this procedure (using a daily diary data set) can be found in Nezlek (2011), and I explain the procedure itself (how to use HLM to do such analyses) in more detail. I must note that I did not develop this technique. I learned about it from reading Bryk and Raudenbush (1992).

The example data sets were designed for the program HLM, and in HLM there is a separate data set for each level of analysis. Slight modifications may be needed for other software packages. In the present case, there are three data sets: a person-level data set, an interaction-level data set, and an item-level data set.

The person-level data set has a contrast code for gender. The interaction-level data set has contrast code (DyadC) indicating if the interaction was a dyad or not. I include these measures simply for illustrative purposes. The diary-level measure of interest is positive active affect, which was measured with three items: happy, excited, and enthusiastic. Participants responded to each item using a 1–7 scale in which 1 represented not at all, and 7 represented strongly. There are five participants (labeled A, B, C, D, and E), who have between three and five interactions each (numbered accordingly), and who provided the three responses mentioned above.

Person-level data set:

ID	Gender
A	1
B	-1
C	1
D	-1
E	-1

Interaction-level data set:

ID	Interaction	DyadC	Happy	Excited	Enthusiastic
A	1	1	5	6	4
A	2	1	3	4	4
A	3	-1	5	5	6
A	4	1	4	5	4
B	1	-1	3	4	3
B	2	-1	4	6	6
B	3	1	2	3	4
C	1	1	6	7	7
C	2	1	5	4	5
C	3	1	3	4	2
C	4	-1	5	6	6
C	5	-1	4	5	6
D	1	1	3	4	4
D	2	1	3	2	4
D	3	1	5	6	6
D	4	-1	4	2	3
E	1	1	4	5	6
E	2	1	5	6	6
E	3	-1	3	4	5

The "trick" in these analyses is to use the interaction-level data set to create an item-level data set so that items can be nested within occasions. This data set is below. In such item-level data files, I typically include a variable to indicate which response an entry represents. In the data set below (variable labeled Index1),

1 indicates happy, 2 excited, and 3 enthusiastic. In the interests of conserving space, I have presented the data for only the first two participants.

Item-level data set:

ID	Interaction	Index1	Response
A	1	1	5
A	1	2	6
A	1	3	4
A	2	1	3
A	2	2	4
A	2	3	4
A	3	1	5
A	3	2	5
A	3	3	6
A	4	1	4
A	4	2	5
A	4	3	4
B	1	1	3
B	1	2	4
B	1	3	3
B	2	1	4
B	2	2	6
B	2	3	6
B	3	1	2
B	3	2	3
B	3	3	4

Listed below is the SPSS syntax to create the item-level data set from the example interaction-level data file. The three responses are read into an item-level file in which the dependent variable of interest is "Response," and the item is represented by the variable Index1. Users need to be cautious when doing this. SPSS writes the item-level file into the active open window, and if the file is simply saved, the original (in this case interaction-level) file can be overwritten. To generate these commands via the "point and click" interface, click on "Data" then "Restructure" and take it from there.

The last command (NULL=KEEP) inserts a row even when there is no valid response for a variable that goes on a certain row. For example, if someone did not provide a rating for happy for an interaction, there would still be three lines of data (three rows) for that interaction for that person. The value for happy (Response for the first line of data) would be missing. The default setting is NULL=DROP. A line of data is not created in the item-level file when the corresponding value is missing. If someone did not provide a rating for happy for an interaction, there would be only two lines of data (two rows) for that interaction for that person. The first line of data would not be in the data set. The presence of such missing data does not affect the estimation algorithm. The program uses all available observations.

```
VARSTOCASES
/MAKE Response FROM Happy Excited Enthusiastic
/INDEX=Index1(3)
/KEEP=ID Interaction
/NULL=KEEP.
```

These data are then joined with the person- and interaction-level data files to create a three-level file. These data are then analyzed with a totally unconditional (null) model in which there are no predictors at any level of analysis. The dependent measure is the variable "Response" (in the item-level file). The model is given below:

Item level	(Level 1)	$y_{ijk} = \pi_{0jk} + e_{ijk}$
Interaction level	(Level 2)	$\pi_{0jk} = \beta_{00k} + r_{0jk}$
Person level	(Level 3)	$\beta_{00k} = \gamma_{000} + u_{00k}$

The item-level reliability of the items (considered as a scale measuring a single construct) is the reliability of the π coefficient. This is the functional equivalent of Cronbach's alpha in a trait-level study. Pure and simple – no more, no less.

As elegant as this technique may be (to borrow a term from our mathematically inclined colleagues), there are limitations and caveats:

1 Assessing reliability in this way requires two measures (items, responses, etc.) of a construct. With only one measure, it is not possible to separate true and random variation, which needs to be done to estimate the reliability. In my experience, I have had more problems with low reliabilities with two-item scales, than with three or more items. As just mentioned, two is the mathematical lower bound for conducting this type of analysis, and unless the items are very well matched, I think analysts will have more difficulty establishing the reliability of two-item scales than for scales with more items. With more items, the idiosyncratic characteristics of the individual items (i.e., variance not attributable to the construct) will have less of an influence on the reliability of the scale.

2 Similar to a standard reliability analysis, all items need to be scored in the same direction. Reverse-scaled items need to be reverse scored before they are entered into the analysis.

3 There are no real diagnostics to help understand why reliability might be low. The program does not produce some type of covariance matrix or factor loadings to help determine which items are not fitting well. One approach that I have found helpful is to calculate correlations between items using a "flat file" – a file that

does not take the nested structure of the data into account. In terms of the present example, this would be the interaction-level data file. Although these correlations confound within- and between-person variability and may not be accurate estimates of within-person relationships (i.e., unconfounded relationships between items), they can provide some hints. If one item had low correlations with the others, I would delete that item from the item-level file and redo the analyses. This can be done easily by selecting records from the item-level file using the index variable. For example, if Enthusiastic (item #3) had low correlations with the other three (which it does not in the sample data set), you could eliminate records from the item-level file that contained responses to this item. For example, in SPSS, you could select cases that meet criteria such as "Index1 NE 3" or "Index1 LT 3." This would leave three responses that could then be analyzed. Moreover, although such diagnostics would seem to be very time consuming, they really are not. Once the data files are set up, within HLM, a new file can be created and analyzed within a matter of minutes – truly. In my experience, once you have acquired the necessary data management skills (explained here), finalizing a multi-item scale administered at the diary level takes about 30 minutes or so – much less if no "cleaning up" is needed. By the way, as a first step, I recommend setting up an item-level file that contains all the items and saving a copy of that file somewhere safe. This way, you do not have to worry about possible mistakes.

4 Although in my experience differences in the size and distribution of variances of different items from a single scale are not pronounced, such differences can influence estimates of reliability. I know of no formal literature describing this (although there may be some), but one way to minimize such influences is to standardize item scores across the entire sample. This sets the total variance of each item to 1.0 and is done from a "flat file." See section on standardizing measures.

5 Although, as described below, it is possible to conduct multivariate, multilevel analyses and to estimate the reliability of several scales simultaneously, I recommend estimating the reliability of each scale (set of responses) individually. In MLM, all parameters are estimated simultaneously, and so reliability estimates for a specific scale will vary as a function of the other scales that are in an analysis. Such differences may not be pronounced, but when analyzed simultaneously, reliability estimates become a type of "conditional" reliability – that is, they reflect the full covariance matrix.

Multivariate analyses

Nesting items within occasions as just discussed is sometimes referred to as adding a "measurement model," and measurement models can be used to conduct multivariate analyses within the multilevel framework. As discussed later, "multivariate" in this case refers more to simultaneous outcomes than to estimating some type of canonical function.

For multivariate analyses, items for a series of constructs are in the same file, with dummy-coded variables used to represent each construct. I will continue the previous example to illustrate how this is done. A more detailed description of this procedure can be found in Nezlek (2011). A discussion of some of the advantages of multivariate MLM can be found in Snijders and Bosker (1999: 201). These include increased statistical power and increased protection against making Type 1 errors.

Assume that for each interaction, in addition to the three items measuring positive active affect (PA) discussed before, positive deactive affect (PD) was also measured with three items: relaxed, content, and satisfied. The interaction-level data file for the first participant would now look like this (the dyad variable has been eliminated to save space):

ID	Interaction	Happy	Excited	Enthusiastic	Relaxed	Content	Satisfied
A	1	5	6	4	3	4	4
A	2	3	4	4	5	4	5
A	3	5	5	6	4	4	6
A	4	4	5	4	3	3	4

The following SPSS commands will generate the necessary item-level file. These commands are the same as those used in the previous example, except that, now, six items are included, and the index has six values instead of three. For convenience's sake, only the data for the first participant are presented.

```
VARSTOCASES
/MAKE Response FROM Happy Excited Enthusiastic Relaxed Content Satisfied
/INDEX=Index1(6)
/KEEP=ID Interaction
/NULL=KEEP.
```

In addition to the data themselves, a dummy code for each of the constructs is needed (as explained below). For the present example, this means a dummy code representing whether a response is a PA item and one representing whether a response is a PD item. The following SPSS commands will do this, and the resulting data for the first participant are below:

```
COMPUTE PA = 0.
COMPUTE PD = 0.
EXECUTE.
IF (Response LE 3) PA=1.
IF (Response GE 4) PD=1.
EXECUTE.
```

Item-level data set:

ID	Interaction	Index1	Response	PA	PD
A	1	1	5	1	0
A	1	2	6	1	0
A	1	3	4	1	0
A	1	4	3	0	1
A	1	5	4	0	1
A	1	6	4	0	1
A	2	1	3	1	0
A	2	2	4	1	0
A	2	3	4	1	0
A	2	4	5	0	1
A	2	5	4	0	1
A	2	6	5	0	1
A	3	1	5	1	0
A	3	2	5	1	0
A	3	3	6	1	0
A	3	4	4	0	1
A	3	5	4	0	1
A	3	6	6	0	1
A	4	1	4	1	0
A	4	2	5	1	0
A	4	3	4	1	0
A	4	4	3	0	1
A	4	5	3	0	1
A	4	6	4	0	1

These data are then analyzed with the following model. The dependent measure is the variable "Response." Note that the level 1 intercept is dropped, and the level 1 predictors (the dummy-coded PA and PD variables) are entered uncentered. See previous section on coding.

Item level	(Level 1)	$y_{ijk} = \pi_{1jk}(PA) + \pi_{2jk}(PD) + e_{ijk}$
Interaction level	(Level 2)	PA: $\pi_{1jk} = \beta_{10k} + r_{1jk}$
		PD: $\pi_{2jk} = \beta_{20k} + r_{2jk}$
Person level	(Level 3)	PA: $\beta_{10k} = \gamma_{100} + u_{10k}$
		PD: $\beta_{20k} = \gamma_{200} + u_{20k}$

When the intercept is dropped and the predictors are entered uncentered, the level 1 coefficients (PA and PD) represent the means for positive active and positive deactive affect respectively. This can be understood by examining predicted values at level 1. For PA items, the dummy-coded predictors are PA = 1 and PD = 0, and the expected value for response is $(\pi_{1jk} * 1) + (\pi_{2jk} * 0)$, or π_{1jk}. For PD items,

PA = 0 and PD = 1, and the expected value for response is $(\pi_{1jk} * 0) + (\pi_{2jk} * 1)$, or π_{2jk}. This is depicted below:

Item-level prediction for PA items $\quad y_{ijk} = \pi_{1jk}(1) + \pi_{2jk}(0) + e_{ijk}$

$$\text{so } y_{ijk} = \pi_{1jk} + e_{ijk}$$

Item-level prediction for PD items $\quad y_{ijk} = \pi_{1jk}(0) + \pi_{2jk}(1) + e_{ijk}$

$$\text{and } y_{ijk} = \pi_{2jk} + e_{ijk}$$

When brought up to level 2 (the interaction level, corresponding to level 1 in analyses without a measurement model), these means represent the latent means for these constructs, and they can be analyzed just as if they were responses per se. The important advantage of setting up such a multivariate model is the ability to compare coefficients across measures. I describe a few such options below.

Perhaps the simplest comparison is between means. For example, a hypothesis that concerns differences in affect (e.g., is the average PA people experience different from the PD?) can be tested by constraining the γ_{100} and γ_{200} coefficients to be the same. If the constraint leads to a poorer fitting model, the means are different. See previous section on comparing coefficients. Note that it is not possible to compare means (statistically) within the multilevel framework without using a measurement model such as this one.

Estimating means for different outcomes in one model also allows statistical comparisons of differences in the strength of relationships between person-level measures and these outcomes. For example, assume a hypothesis concerns the possibility that Extraversion is related more strongly to PA than it is to PD. The level 3 (person-level) model is below. The level 1 and level 2 models are not depicted. They are the same as those in the previous model.

Person level $\quad$ (Level 3) $\quad$ PA: $\beta_{10k} = \gamma_{100} + \gamma_{101}(\text{Extra}) + u_{10k}$

$$\text{PD: } \beta_{20k} = \gamma_{200} + \gamma_{201}(\text{Extra}) + u_{20k}$$

Relationships between Extraversion and PA are represented by the γ_{101} coefficient, and relationships between Extraversion and PD are represented by the γ_{201} coefficient. The strength of these two relationships can be compared by constraining these two coefficients to be equal. Although relationships between a person-level measure such as extraversion and PA and PD could be examined separately (and tested individually for significance) without using a measurement model, the strength of these relationships could not be compared statistically. The multivariate approach described here provides the ability to test the individual relationships (the significance of the γ_{101} and γ_{102} coefficients per se), while it provides the added benefit of being able to compare them.

Predictors can also be added to the interaction-level model, and these coefficients can be compared. Assume a hypothesis concerns differences between dyads and non-dyads, with an additional interest that the two types of interactions will differ more in terms of PD than PA. Dyads can be represented by a contrast variable, DyadC, as described previously, and this contrast variable would be entered at level 2 (uncentered), as depicted below. The level 1 model is not depicted.

Interaction level	(Level 2)	PA: $\pi_{1jk} = \beta_{10k} + \beta_{11k}(\text{DyadC}) + r_{1jk}$
		PD: $\pi_{2jk} = \beta_{20k} + \beta_{21k}(\text{DyadC}) + r_{2jk}$
Person level	(Level 3)	PA: $\beta_{10k} = \gamma_{100} + u_{10k}$
		PA DyadC: $\beta_{11k} = \gamma_{110} + u_{11k}$
		PD: $\beta_{20k} = \gamma_{200} + u_{20k}$
		PA DyadC: $\beta_{21k} = \gamma_{210} + u_{21k}$

Differences between dyads and non-dyads are now represented by the γ_{110} and γ_{210} coefficients, the DyadC coefficients for PA and PD respectively. The "dyad effect" for these measures can be compared by constraining these two coefficients to be equal. Moreover, such an analysis also tests the dyad effect for each outcome, the significance of the γ_{110} and γ_{210} coefficients per se. Similar to the person-level relationships between extraversion and affect I just described, the dyad effect for PA and for PD can be estimated in separate analyses that do not require a measurement model; however, unless these coefficients are estimated in the same model, they cannot be compared.

Just as it was possible to compare relationships between Extraversion and mean PA to relationships between Extraversion and mean PD, differences in the strength of relationships between Extraversion and the dyad effects for these two outcomes can be compared. The person level-model is depicted below. The critical coefficients are the γ_{111} and γ_{211} coefficients, representing the relationships between Extraversion and the dyad effect for PA and PD respectively. Their equality can be tested by examining the impact on model fit of constraining them to be equal.

Person level	PA Intercept:	$\beta_{10k} = \gamma_{100} + \gamma_{101}(\text{Extra}) + u_{10k}$
	PA DyadC:	$\beta_{11k} = \gamma_{110} + \gamma_{111}(\text{Extra}) + u_{11k}$
	PD Intercept:	$\beta_{20k} = \gamma_{200} + \gamma_{201}(\text{Extra}) + u_{20k}$
	PA DyadC:	$\beta_{21k} = \gamma_{210} + \gamma_{211}(\text{Extra}) + u_{21k}$

As discussed in the section on coding, categorical predictors can also be represented with a series of dummy codes, one code representing each of the categories. Such dummy coding provides separate parameter estimates for each category, in contrast to contrast coding, which estimates difference scores. At the interaction level, separate estimates for PA and PD in dyads and non-dyads could be estimated with the following model. The dummy codes Dyad (1 = dyad, 0 = no dyad) and Non-Dyad (1 = non-dyad, 0 = dyad) are entered uncentered, and the intercept is dropped.

Interaction level PA: $\pi_{1jk} = \beta_{11k}(\text{Dyad}) + \beta_{12k}(\text{Non-Dyad}) + r_{1jk}$

PD: $\pi_{2jk} = \beta_{21k}(\text{Dyad}) + \beta_{22k}(\text{Non-Dyad}) + r_{2jk}$

Person level PA Dyad: $\beta_{11k} = \gamma_{110} + u_{11k}$

PA Non-Dyad: $\beta_{12k} = \gamma_{120} + u_{12k}$

PD Dyad: $\beta_{21k} = \gamma_{210} + u_{21k}$

PD Non-Dyad: $\beta_{22k} = \gamma_{220} + u_{22k}$

Such a model allows for comparing PA and PD for dyads only and for non-dyads only. The first comparison involves the γ_{110} and γ_{210} coefficients, and the second involves the γ_{120} and γ_{220} coefficients. To complete the example, person-level predictors can be added to these models to test hypotheses involving differences in the strength of relationships between PA and PD in dyads and non-dyads and individual differences such as extraversion. See below. By now, you should know which coefficients to compare.

Person level PA Dyad: $\beta_{11k} = \gamma_{110} + \gamma_{111}(\text{Extra}) + u_{11k}$

PA Non-Dyad: $\beta_{12k} = \gamma_{120} + \gamma_{121}(\text{Extra}) + u_{12k}$

PD Dyad: $\beta_{21k} = \gamma_{210} + \gamma_{211}(\text{Extra}) + u_{21k}$

PD Non-Dyad: $\beta_{22k} = \gamma_{220} + \gamma_{221}(\text{Extra}) + u_{22k}$

For the sake of thoroughness, I will provide a brief example of how a multivariate MLM might be used in an interval contingent study, such as a daily diary study. Assume that negative deactive affect (e.g., sad) and negative active affect (e.g., anxious) are measured each day with three items each. Participants also provide a description of the negative social events (e.g., an argument) and negative achievement events (e.g., task failure) that occurred each day. A basic model that would allow examining differences in the strength of the relationships between these two types of events and the two types of negative affect is provided below. Social (negative social event scores) and Achieve (negative achievement event scores) are entered group-mean centered at the day level.

Item level $\quad y_{ijk} = \pi_{1jk}(NA) + \pi_{2jk}(ND) + e_{ijk}$

Day level $\quad NA: \pi_{1jk} = \beta_{10k} + \beta_{11k}(Social) + \beta_{12k}(Achieve) + r_{1jk}$

$\quad\quad\quad\quad\; ND: \pi_{2jk} = \beta_{20k} + \beta_{21k}(Social) + \beta_{22k}(Achieve) + r_{2jk}$

Person level $\quad$ NA Intercept: $\quad \beta_{10k} = \gamma_{100} + u_{10k}$

$\quad\quad\quad\quad\quad\;$ NA Social: $\quad\quad \beta_{11k} = \gamma_{110} + u_{11k}$

$\quad\quad\quad\quad\quad\;$ NA Achieve: $\quad\; \beta_{12k} = \gamma_{120} + u_{12k}$

$\quad\quad\quad\quad\quad\;$ ND Intercept: $\quad \beta_{20k} = \gamma_{200} + u_{20k}$

$\quad\quad\quad\quad\quad\;$ ND Social: $\quad\quad \beta_{21k} = \gamma_{210} + u_{21k}$

$\quad\quad\quad\quad\quad\;$ ND Achieve: $\quad\; \beta_{22k} = \gamma_{220} + u_{21k}$

So, if a researcher believed that social stress influenced ND (depression) more than it influenced NA (anxiety), the γ_{110} and γ_{210} coefficients (slopes) could be compared. Similar comparisons could be made for achievement-related stress by comparing the γ_{120} and γ_{220} coefficients. By now, you should have the hang of all this and should recognize that individual differences such as anxiety, depression, extraversion, neuroticism, and so forth can be added as predictors to the person-level model, and differences in the strength of these relationships can be compared in a whole bunch of ways.

The ability of multivariate MLM to compare slopes involving different outcome measures can provide important advantages over a series of MLM analyses of individual variables. As noted previously, relationships that involve different outcomes cannot be compared statistically if they are estimated in separate analyses. This may not be a problem if the results of univariate analyses find that the slope for one outcome is significant, whereas the same slope for another is not. If both slopes are significant, then questions about whether they are different can arise. Moreover, a test of the significance of the difference between a significant and non-significant slope is more compelling than simply noting one is significant and the other is not.

Nevertheless, certain caveats are in order for multivariate MLM:

1 Modeling multiple outcomes requires at least two measures (items, responses, etc.) for each construct. As noted above, in my experience three items are better than two, and four is somewhat better than three. Moreover, because the algorithm relies on the entire covariance matrix and estimates all covariance simultaneously, the number of items per scale should be as similar as possible. If one scale has many more items than the others (e.g., 10 vs. 3), the covariances involving the scale with more items will influence the resulting covariances (all of them) more than scales with fewer items.
2 As discussed in the section on comparing coefficients, although significance tests of individual coefficients are invariant under transformation, differences in the

covariances of measures will affect significance tests of the differences of coefficients (i.e., the constraints just described). To minimize the influence differing covariances will have on comparisons of coefficients, researchers should try to maximize the similarity of the variances of the scales they use in multivariate analyses. One way to do this is to use the same response scale (e.g., 1–7) for all measures and items. If this is not possible (e.g., the data have been collected), the items can be normalized across the entire sample before analysis.

3   As described above for a reliability analysis, all items need to be scored in the same direction. Moreover, although you can obtain reliability estimates for individual measures within a multivariate analysis, these reliabilities will be "conditional" reliabilities. Conditional in this sense refers to the fact that the estimates of the reliabilities of each measure will incorporate the variances and covariances (and reliabilities) of the other measures.

4   Similarly, although the covariances among the random error terms of the intercepts can be used to estimate the correlations between scales (e.g., the Tau(pi) matrix in the program HLM), I urge analysts to be cautious in interpreting these correlations. As was the case with reliabilities (described in the previous chapter), these covariances are conditional, and deleting or including additional constructs can change the estimated correlation (covariance) between two constructs. For example, if one measured NA, ND, PA, and PD with three items each and included all four scales in a single analysis, the estimated correlation between PA and PD might be different from the correlation estimated if only PA and PD were included in the model. This is because the covariances are between error terms, which are estimated.

5   Unlike some OLS-based multivariate techniques (e.g., discriminant analysis, canonical correlation), it is not possible to obtain some type of estimate of the best fitting combination of items or measures. Within the dummy-coded system I have described, all items receive the same weight, and coefficients for each measure reflect relationships between that measure and predictors of interest.

Lagged analyses

As many experimentalists are all too eager to point out, most diary studies provide correlational data, which (at least to them) means that one makes causal inferences at one's own peril. Putting aside such narrow-mindedness, one way to address questions of causality with correlational data is to perform lagged analyses. Resting on the assumption that causes precede effects, the logic of such analyses is that if x at time n is related to y at time $n + 1$, then x can be considered to be a possible cause of y. More sophisticated models or approaches take into account (simultaneously) the possibility that y at time n is related to x at time $n + 1$.

When both possibilities are considered simultaneously, this is sometimes called a "cross-lagged analysis." The "cross" refers to the fact that if the data are diagrammed with x and y at time n on the far left, and x and y at time $n + 1$ on the far right, a line from x_n to y_n+_1 crosses a line from y_n to x_n+_1. Exactly how to conduct cross-lagged analyses for single level data has been the topic of considerable discussion over the years. It seems that the current best practice is to use some type of SEM because this allows for better control of error covariances. Unfortunately, as I write this volume, I know of no formal, rigorous technique that has been developed to conduct cross-lagged analyses within the multilevel framework. Nevertheless, it is possible to do lagged analyses within the multilevel framework, and, for the moment, the presently available methods will need to suffice.

I illustrate this technique by describing some analyses presented in Nezlek (2002). Participants in the study provided daily measures of anxiety (anx) and private self-awareness (aka private self-consciousness, prv). The hypotheses of interest concerned causal relationships between anxiety and self-awareness. In the first equation, the lag from anxiety on day $n - 1$ to private self-awareness on day n is estimated, and, in the second equation, the lag from private self-awareness on day $n - 1$ to anxiety on day n is estimated. The lagged coefficients are, respectively, $\beta_{2j}(\text{anx day } n - 1)$ in the first equation and $\beta_{1j}(\text{prv day } n - 1)$ in the second equation:

$$\text{prv(day } n)_{ij} = \beta_{0j} + \beta_{1j}(\text{prv day } n - 1) + \beta_{2j}(\text{anx day } n - 1) + r_{ij}$$

$$\text{anx(day } n)_{ij} = \beta_{0j} + \beta_{1j}(\text{prv day } n - 1) + \beta_{2j}(\text{anx day } n - 1) + r_{ij}$$

The results of these analyses were clear. The $\beta_{2j}(\text{anx day } n - 1)$ coefficient in the first equation, which represented the lag from anxiety to self-awareness, was significant ($p < .05$). In contrast, the $\beta_{1j}(\text{prv day } n - 1)$ coefficient in the second equation, which represented the lag from self-awareness to anxiety, was not significant ($t < 1$). Such a pattern suggested that increases in anxiety led to increases in private self-awareness, whereas increases in self-awareness did not lead to increases in anxiety.

The following commands can be used in SPSS to create lagged variables for a daily diary study. The commands assume that records are individual days and are sorted first within person (id) and then within each person by time (jdate – see section on temporal indicators for a discussion). In this example, a lag of 1 is used. A lag of 1 is indicated by the "1" in the parentheses following the "LAG" command. Longer lags can be created by changing this parameter. In this file, id is a string variable (not important for present purposes) and jdate is a numeric variable. The two example variables are anxiety (anx) and the negative events that occurred each day (negevent).

/* The first set of commands creates a variable, jdateprev, which represents the date of the previous (lagged) record, but only for cases in which the id of the present record and the id of the lagged record are the same. If the id of the present record and the lagged record are not the same, jdateprev is missing. This is done to avoid creating lagged variables across participants, i.e., the last day (record) for person 1 and the first (day) record for person 2. */

```
IF (id = LAG(id,1)) jdateprev=LAG(jdate,1).
EXECUTE.
```

/* The second set of commands creates a lagged variable for anxiety (anxprev) only for consecutive days for the same person, i.e., when jdate = jdateprev + 1. If this condition is not met, anxprev is set to missing. Keep in mind that jdateprev is missing for adjacent records from different people. */

```
IF (jdate = jdateprev + 1) anxprev=lag(anx,1).
EXECUTE.
```

/* These commands create a lagged variable for negative events (negevprev) under the same conditions as for anxiety. */

```
IF (jdate = jdateprev + 1) negevprev=lag(negevent,1).
EXECUTE.
```

/* If you prefer, you can eliminate records that do not have a previous day with the following commands. This makes it easier to generate descriptive statistics for the data that are used for lagged analyses. */

```
FILTER OFF.
USE ALL.
SELECT IF (jdate = jdateprev+1).
EXECUTE.
```

These variables can then be used to do analyses that are structurally similar to the analyses I presented before, with the obvious difference that causal relationships are now between anxiety and negative events. The primary shortcoming of such analyses is the inability to compare statistically the x–y and y–x lags. If one lag is significant and the other is not, that is reasonable support for concluding that the causal relationship flows in the direction represented by the significant lag and not in the other direction. What if both lags are significant, but one is larger than the other? The two coefficients cannot be compared statistically because they come from different analyses. If the two coefficients are similar in size, such questions are moot, but what is similar, and what if they are prima facie different (e.g., .2 vs. 1.5)? Unfortunately, at present, analysts will have to live with these limitations.

A few caveats are in order. First, the time between points must be the same for consecutive observations. In interval contingent studies, this is relatively easy to determine. If you are doing a daily study, Monday provides the $n - 1$ data for Tuesday, Tuesday provides the $n - 1$ data for Wednesday, and so forth. If data collection occasions are randomly selected (e.g., a beeper study), the time between measurement occasions may be sufficiently different as to call into question their functional equivalence. One might feel comfortable treating 75- and 90-minute lags as functionally the same, whereas it might not be so easy to treat 30- and 120-minute lags as functionally equivalent.

In an event contingent study, equal spacing between events is probably unlikely. For example, for most people, social interactions do not occur at regularly spaced intervals (or even roughly regularly spaced). Moreover, if the events are of meaningfully unequal lengths (e.g., 15-minute vs. 90-minute interactions), it is not clear to me exactly how the lag is defined – from end to beginning, from middle to middle? There may be exceptions to this. For example, sexual interactions may occur in the evening on some type of regular basis.

One way of dealing with unequal spacing of observations is to ignore it. Depending upon the structure of the data, this may not be a fatal error, e.g., in a beeper study in which the intervals between observations are not too different. Even if the time between observations is very different, one may want to assume that measures collected at occasion $n - 1$ represent causes of measures collected at occasion n. For example, a researcher may be interested in causes represented by statements such as "the last time this happened."

Regardless of the assumptions one makes about the time between occasions of measurement, analysts need to describe these assumptions and describe the number of observations and the length of time between observations used in an analysis. Analysts also need to keep in mind that the number of observations that can be used for lagged analyses will necessarily be less than that which can be used for static analyses. Even assuming regular and equally spaced interval data, the first and last observations in a data set cannot be used in lagged analyses. If you are examining one-day lags, if someone is missing a day, there is no lag for that day to the next.

Finally, there is the issue of between-person differences in lagged relationships. Just as within-person coefficients representing static relationships can vary as a function of person-level differences, coefficients representing lagged relationships can vary. It is also possible that even if the mean coefficient representing a lagged relationship is not significantly different from 0, there may be individual differences in these coefficients such that the lag is significant for some people but not for others.

Non-standard error structures including autocorrelation

Although there may not be a consensus as to what constitutes a "standard" error structure in MLM, for present purposes this will mean the following: (1) that a random effect is estimated for all slopes; (2) that all of the covariances between these random effects are estimated; and (3) errors at the diary level are uncorrelated.

Estimating random effects for individual slopes was discussed before in the section on modeling error, and I will not repeat myself. In terms of (2), the default in most programs is to estimate all the covariances among the random effects that are estimated. Moreover, there is considerable variability across programs in how much the covariances among errors can be controlled. For example, in the program HLM, all covariances are estimated, whereas in the program MLwiN, an analyst can fix certain covariances. Regardless, such matters are beyond the scope of this volume and are not central to the concerns of most diary researchers.

Numerous analysts are concerned, however, with correlations between measures taken from the same person, typically referred to as autocorrelation (or auto-covariance). Another term is autoregressive, and such relationships are often discussed in terms of how far apart observations are. For example, the error between adjacent observations can be modeled (a lag of 1), or between observations separated by another observation (a lag of 2), and so forth.

Before discussing the application of autoregressive error structures to the types of diary data that are typically collected by social and personality psychologists, I think it is informative to describe the types of research questions and data structures for which autoregressive models were initially intended. Modeling autoregressive errors arose from concerns about the accuracy of estimates from what have generally been called "time series analyses."

I will note a few characteristics about the data in a "typical" time series analysis. The typical data structure in a time series analysis has many data points, perhaps 50 to 100 or more – more than is collected in the typical diary study. For example, time series analysis has been used to model monthly or quarterly changes in unemployment over many years, perhaps decades. In addition, the focus of time series analysis is often the trends or cycles in such data. For example, one hears of "seasonally adjusted" unemployment figures, referring to unemployment estimates that take into account the fact that unemployment has a cyclical component. Sometimes such cycles are examined using what is called Fourier analysis, which decomposes a set of data into different cycles, combinations of sine and cosine waves. Estimating such cycles can require numerous observations. For example, to examine an annual cycle, 50 months of observations would provide a basis to estimate just over four cycles. Finally, although many applications of time series analysis involve only one set of observations (e.g., unemployment in the USA), the time series of different groups can be compared (multi-group time series analysis). Typically, the number of groups in a multi-group time series analysis is rather small, much smaller than the number of participants in the typical diary study. In addition, the data are well structured. The same number of observations is collected for each group at the same time.

I mention this to make the point that the importance of modeling autoregressive errors was established (initially) for data structures and research questions that are different from those in play for many diary studies conducted by social and personality psychologists. Moreover, to model autoregressive errors, the data have to be well structured. The time between adjacent observations needs to be the same (or at least functionally the same). This leaves out any event contingent study, such as a social interaction diary study, in which the number of observations and the spacing of adjacent observations vary between persons, and the spacing varies within persons. It also leaves out random, signal contingent studies in which the spacing between adjacent observations intentionally varies within a person, and schedules of data collection intentionally vary between persons, unless of course, you chose to ignore this.

This leaves only studies in which the data are collected on a regular basis that is the same for all participants. This is typically referred to as a fixed design. Moreover, missing data are not allowed, and for a set of observations to be retained, any missing values need to be replaced. Current thinking suggests that some type of imputation is best. Furthermore, technically speaking, the data should be collected at the same time (e.g., across the same days) for all participants. This provides a basis for controlling (or at least holding constant) exogenous effects across participants. Given that such effects are typically not of interest (e.g., the weather each day), at least for estimating autoregressive error terms, this rule can be observed in the breach.

Assuming your data can run this gauntlet, you can model autoregressive effects with different lags (adjacent, 2, 3, whatever strikes your fancy). Regardless, my sense is that most social and personality psychologists are probably interested in a lag of 1 (adjacent observations), but your needs may be different. Moreover, exactly how this is done varies from program to program.

Noting all this, I have not read an article published by a social and personality psychologist in which it was reported that modeling autoregressive error led to meaningfully different conclusions than when autoregressive error was not modeled. When I use the term "meaningfully different conclusions" I am referring to tests of fixed effects, which are typically the focus of most hypotheses. This is not to say that modeling autoregressive errors has not been shown to lead to better model fits. Often it does, but given that, often, the data need to be forced a bit to fit the fixed effects model, the benefits of modeling autoregressive error fit may not offset the costs. Note also that I have not read anything close to every article written by a social or personality psychologist describing a diary study, and it is possible that fitting an autoregressive model did make a difference in terms of the substantive conclusions, but authors did not note this. If there are studies with such findings, I am certain someone will point this out in a review of this volume or some time during a convention somewhere.

Regardless, my guess is that when thinking of autocorrelation, most diary researchers are interested in controlling for some type of linear trend in their data. If an observation is increasing across time, there would be a positive autocorrelation, whereas if it were decreasing, there would be a negative autocorrelation. One way to control for such trends without modeling autocorrelated error is to include a predictor at level 1 (the diary level) representing time. This would control for the possibility that a within-person covariance between two measures collected across time did not reflect the simple linear trend in each. For example, if two measures rely on checklists, and, over time, if participants simply tire of checking items, there will be a positive relationship between the two measures. Controlling for the time would eliminate such a relationship. Moreover, non-linear trends can also be modeled in this way. See West et al. (2011) for a brief discussion of modeling temporal trends in longitudinal data.

I realize that some of what I have written here does not agree with what others have suggested about the importance of autocorrelation. To some extent, this difference may reflect a difference in emphasis on modeling per se and on the substantive conclusions a model supports. As I mentioned previously, modeling autocorrelated error (when appropriate) often leads to a better fitting model but may not provide different estimates of fixed effects, which are invariably the effects of interest.

Comparing relationships across time and panel designs

Although such use may not be common, if diary data are collected on repeated occasions, perhaps as part of a panel design, such data can be analyzed within the multilevel framework. For simplicity's sake, assume that people participate in a daily diary study and provide diary-level and trait-level data twice, once in April and once in October. I will describe procedures that can be used to address two types of questions:

1 Is the relationship between a person-level measure and a diary-level measure (intercept or slope) consistent across time? In the panel design nomenclature, such relationships are sometimes referred to as synchronous relationships.
2 Is the relationship between a person-level measure at time 1 and a diary-level measure at time 2 different from the relationship between the same person-level measure at time 2 and the same diary measure at time 1? In the panel design nomenclature, these are sometimes referred to as cross-lagged relationships, and differences in such cross-lagged relationships can be used to support causal inferences.

I describe a procedure using the program HLM. The modeling techniques per se are not limited to or specific to HLM, simply preparing the data in two files is peculiar to HLM. First, the data for both time periods are merged into a single file, one for the person-level measures and one for the diary data. The person-level measures for the two data collection periods are distinguished, Anxiety1, Anxiety2, and so forth. For the diary data, each record (each day) is assigned two dummy-codes, Time1 and Time2. For the diary data collected in April, Time1 = 1 and Time2 = 0, and for the diary data collected in October, Time1 = 0 and Time2 = 1. If you want to include level 1 predictors, you will need to multiply each daily measure by each dummy code, creating two variables for each measure. For present purposes, I will use a measure of daily stress, which when multiplied by the dummy codes will produce two measures, Stress1 and Stress2.

For this example, I will focus on one person-level measure, trait anxiety, which is labeled Anxiety1 and Anxiety2. The outcome measure is self-esteem. Synchronous relationships between means of diary measures and person-level measures can be compared using the following analysis. Note that in the level 1 model, the intercept is deleted and the dummy-coded predictors are entered uncentered. The synchronous relationships for Time1 and Time2 are represented (respectively) by the γ_{11}(Anxiety1) term in the first person-level equation and the γ_{21}(Anxiety2) term in the second person level equation:

Day level $\qquad y_{ij} = \beta_{1j}(\text{Time1}) + \beta_{2j}(\text{Time2}) + r_{ij}$

Person level $\qquad \beta_{1j} = \gamma_{10} + \gamma_{11}(\text{Anxiety1}) + \mu_{1j}$

$\qquad\qquad\qquad \beta_{2j} = \gamma_{20} + \gamma_{21}(\text{Anxiety2}) + \mu_{2j}$

The level 1 model can be expanded by adding predictors for each time period. Assuming the predictor is stress, this would lead to the following day-level model. In this model, the intercept is deleted, the dummy-coded Time1 and Time2 variables are entered uncentered (as before), and Stress1 and Stress2 can be entered centered (group-mean centered for me):

$$y_{ij} = \beta_{1j}(\text{Time1}) + \beta_{2j}(\text{Time2}) + \beta_{3j}(\text{Stress1}) + \beta_{4j}(\text{Stress2}) + r_{ij}$$

The synchronous moderating relationships between anxiety and the stress slope can be compared within the context of the following person-level model. The critical coefficients are the γ_{31}(Anxiety1) term in the third equation and the γ_{41}(Anxiety2) term in the fourth equation. Constraining them to be equal tests the similarity of the synchronous relationships between anxiety and the slope for stress.

$$\beta_{1j} = \gamma_{10} + \gamma_{11}(\text{Anxiety1}) + \mu_{1j}$$
$$\beta_{2j} = \gamma_{20} + \gamma_{21}(\text{Anxiety2}) + \mu_{2j}$$
$$\beta_{3j} = \gamma_{30} + \gamma_{31}(\text{Anxiety1}) + \mu_{3j}$$
$$\beta_{4j} = \gamma_{40} + \gamma_{41}(\text{Anxiety2}) + \mu_{4j}$$

With these models as a context, examining the cross-lagged relationships is relatively straightforward. For analyses of means for diary measures, the following models can be used. Such an analysis might be interesting to examine relationships between daily stressors (now the outcome variable) and dispositional anxiety. A significant γ_{12}(Anxiety2) term in the first person-level equation would indicate that changes in daily stressors lead to changes in dispositional anxiety. A significant γ_{21}(Anxiety1) term in the second person-level equation would indicate that changes in dispositional anxiety lead to changes in daily stressors. Moreover, the strength of these lagged relationships can be compared by constraining these coefficients to be equal.

Day level $\qquad y_{ij} = \beta_{1j}(\text{Time1}) + \beta_{2j}(\text{Time2}) + r_{ij}$

Person level $\quad \beta_{1j} = \gamma_{10} + \gamma_{11}(\text{Anxiety1}) + \gamma_{12}(\text{Anxiety2}) + \mu_{1j}$

$\qquad\qquad\qquad \beta_{2j} = \gamma_{20} + \gamma_{21}(\text{Anxiety1}) + \gamma_{22}(\text{Anxiety2}) + \mu_{2j}$

Analysis of dyads

The dyad is a popular topic for social and personality psychologists, particularly for those interested in personal relationships. Unfortunately, the statistical issues raised in studying dyads are particularly complex and are beyond the scope of this book. Interested readers can consult Kenny, Kashy, and Cook (2006) for advice. Nevertheless, I can offer some guidance. A critical aspect of analyzing dyadic data (diaries included) is whether the members of the dyad are distinguishable or not. The prototypical example of a distinguishable dyad is a husband and wife, and the prototypical example of a non-distinguishable dyad is a dyad consisting of two same-sex friends.

When dyads are distinguishable, parameters for each type of person in the dyad can be estimated separately, and person-level predictors for each type of person can be included. For example, assume a daily diary study of husbands and wives with anxiety as an outcome and stress as a predictor. For each day, two entries are made, one for the husband and one for the wife. A critical component of such an analysis is creating a dummy code to distinguish husband and wife data and multiplying the husband's and the wife's data for each day by these dummy codes. See Barnett, Marshall, Raudenbush, and Brennan (1993) for an example of this technique.

Using the no-intercept models described before, this would produce the day-level model below. In essence, a separate model is estimated for husbands, with β_{1j} as the intercept and β_{3j} as the slope for stress, and, for wives, with β_{2j} as the intercept and β_{4j} as the slope for stress:

$$y_{ij} = \beta_{1j}(\text{Husband}) + \beta_{2j}(\text{Wife}) + \beta_{3j}(\text{Husband-Stress}) + \beta_{4j}(\text{Wife-Stress}) + r_{ij}$$

This model also provides a framework in which husbands' and wives' intercepts and slopes can be modeled as a function of either husband or wife person-level variable such as neuroticism. Of course, such coefficients can be compared using tests of fixed effects.

$$\text{Husband-stress: } \beta_{3j} = \gamma_{30} + \gamma_{31}(\text{Husband-Neuroticism}) + \gamma_{32}(\text{Wife-Neuroticism}) + \mu_{1j}$$

The analysis of non-distinguishable dyads is more challenging than the analysis of distinguishable dyads. Given the present understanding of the modeling techniques involved, I offer the following. The best way to analyze such data is to conduct a three-level model in which days of measurement are nested within persons and persons are nested within dyads. This provides the ability to model person-level relationships (now at level 2 out of three levels) while controlling for the dependence of observations collected within each dyad.

Such a model will tax the carrying capacity of a data set because there are only two observations at the intermediate level (now the person level). As you evaluate your data's ability to estimate all the errors in this three-level model, you may need to make decisions about which error terms are more important. Given the likely data structure in such a study (e.g., 10–15 days of diary data for 25–50 dyads; of course, more is better), my guess is that you will have the most difficulty estimating slopes of moderating relationships at the person level. For example, this would include dyad-level analyses of relationships between a person-level variable such as neuroticism and a day-level slope between stress and anxiety. In such cases, you can fix the dyad-level effect (i.e., eliminate the error term in the dyad-level equation).

Although some reviewers may cry "foul," you may want to consider ignoring the dyadic level of analysis. That is, simply treat individuals as if they were not members of dyads. After all, some type of nesting is ignored in virtually all studies. Nonetheless, this could be defended if and only if the following conditions are met (at the least):

1   You have no hypotheses involving measures at the dyad level such as how long the members of the dyad have known each other.
2   You have no hypotheses involving measures about the dyad itself such as how much the members of the dyad like each other.
3   You cannot estimate any of the dyad-level error terms.

If a study focuses on dyads, it seems unlikely that conditions 1 and 2 will hold. Why study dyads if you have no hypotheses about them? Nevertheless, you may have data that were collected within dyads that you are analyzing with a different set of hypotheses in mind. You could make a statistically based argument (condition 3), but my guess is that you might be able to estimate the random error term for the intercept. You can just about always estimate the random effect for the intercept. As a fallback position, you could analyze the data both ways and see if there are any differences. Keep in mind that MLM is about incorporating dependencies in a data structure; if there are no dependencies (if dyads do not matter) a less complex model may be appropriate. Editors and reviewers may have difficulty appreciating such an argument, and, if they do, simply present the three-level model and move on.

I will note that such a three-level model is not without its detractors. For example, Kenny et al. (2006: 347) specifically recommend not doing this. Although I think their argument has some merit, I do not think that the modeling technique they recommend is appropriate. Kenny et al. recommend assigning a dummy code (0, 1) to one of the members of a dyad and then analyzing the data as if the dyads were distinguishable (e.g., male and female). To me, this is puzzling because it is unclear how one member can be assigned a 0 and the other assigned a 1. More important, the results of the analyses will vary as a function of which member gets a 0 and which gets a 1. In essence, all the 0s are considered as a group and all the 1s are considered as a comparison group. Given that the members of the dyads are (by definition) indistinguishable, any assignment is arbitrary, and, by extension, any set of parameters that are estimated is arbitrary.

My concerns about the appropriateness of their approach is reflected in their concern that the three-level model I discussed above does not allow for a negative relationship between the means for members of a dyad. The model provides a basis for estimating only a variance (without a sign). As I understand the situation, without the ability to classify members unambiguously, it is not possible to estimate a signed (positive or negative) relationship between the means. For example, in a simple non-diary study in which I measured the attitudes of married couples, I could calculate the correlation (Pearson's r) between attitudes of husbands and wives. Each couple would have two measures, and a correlation could be calculated at the couple level. Such a correlation could be either positive or negative. In contrast, if the members of a dyad were not distinguishable, a correlation could not be calculated. One would be limited to computing an intraclass correlation, which, as a measure of variance, is constrained to be positive.

Noting all this, Kenny et al. do make an important point when they note that a three-level mode such as I discuss does not take into account that days are actually "crossed" rather than nested. This refers to the fact that the model does not take advantage of the information provided by the fact that day 1 for person 1 in dyad 1 is the same as day 1 for person on 2 in dyad 1. At present, I know of no modeling technique that can do this. My sense is that it is more conservative to assume that days are nested rather than crossed (i.e., crossed data are more structured than nested data). Therefore, a three-level model in which the data are treated as nested is a conservative approach that avoids the more serious problems associated with assigning dummy codes on an arbitrary basis.

At present, I can offer advice about only interval contingent studies. I do not know of any systematic treatment of event contingent studies such as social interaction diary studies. The difficulty in analyzing such data is that people will have interactions with others with whom the other member of the dyad will not (distinguishable or indistinguishable dyads). When members of the dyad are interacting with each other, such interactions could be nested within the dyad (with days as an intervening level or not), and analyses similar to those just described could be conducted. The limitation of such analyses is that they do not include the interactions members of a dyad have with people outside of their dyad, interactions which will not overlap. Researchers will need to make decisions about analytic strategies based upon their hypotheses of interest.

Finally, as you might imagine from the foregoing, how to analyze dyadic data within the context of diary studies is an issue that seems to be far from resolved. I have made recommendations based upon my understanding of the logic and underlying rationale for MLM. You may find other approaches more to your liking. Regardless of how you decide to analyze your data, I urge you to examine carefully the assumptions underlying the analytic framework you select. It can make a difference.

7

Other data analytic strategies: Measures of instability

The MLM analyses I just described focus on covariances. For example, how are two diary-level measures, x and y, related, and does this relationship vary as a function of some individual difference? Although such analyses are commonly used (and appear to be increasing in popularity), there are other ways of conceptualizing and analyzing the data generated in diary studies. One important alternative is to examine variability per se. How much, and in what ways, do people vary across occasions of measurement?

An important rationale for studying variability per se is the belief/assumption that high levels of instability represent some type of psychological distress. For example, most conceptualizations of neuroticism include some aspect of instability (sometimes described as lability). Within such a framework, within-person variability is an indicator of psychological adjustment.

Standard deviation

Perhaps the most straightforward way of measuring instability is the within-person standard deviation. In such analyses, each participant's data are treated separately, and the standard deviation of a measure is calculated and used in analyses in combination with other person-level measures. Although not typically associated with diary studies per se, perhaps the best example of this is Kernis's work on the instability of self-esteem (e.g., Kernis, 2005). The upshot of this research is that although level of self-esteem (mean self-esteem across occasions) is negatively related to the instability of self-esteem (the standard deviation across occasions), the instability of self-esteem is a meaningfully distinct construct from level of self-esteem (dispositional self-esteem). Eid and Diener (1999) also present an argument for using within-person standard deviations as a measure of instability.

Although the instability of self-esteem (or other measures) may reflect some type of general instability rather than the instability of self-esteem per se (e.g., Gable & Nezlek, 1998), the gist of this research is that instability can be measured simply by calculating the variance across occasions of measurement. Such measures can be calculated using some type of aggregation algorithm, which is available in most statistical packages. For example, in SPSS, click on "Data" then "Aggregate" and then on "Function" and select "Standard deviation."

A somewhat more sophisticated approach to measuring within-person variability was proposed by Fleeson (2001). Fleeson calculated within-person standard deviations and within-person measures of skew and kurtosis. Although the results of this study were complex, skew and kurtosis appeared to represent characteristics of within-person variability that were different from those represented by standard deviations. The ease with which skew and kurtosis can be calculated will vary from statistical package to statistical package, but interested analysts should be able to convince the package they use to calculate these measures.

Flux, pulse, spin

A way of measuring within-person variability that is meaningfully different from the types of within-person measures just described was proposed by Moskowitz and Zuroff (2004). A distinctive feature of this approach is that it presupposes that responses and, by implication, variability can be represented in a multidimensional space such as the affective or interpersonal circumplex. They proposed measures of what they labeled as flux, pulse, and spin to describe within-person variability within such a multidimensional space, which in their case was the interpersonal circumplex (e.g., Wiggins, 1991).

Moskowitz and Zuroff collected data describing an individual's interpersonal behaviors during social interactions. Using a checklist, participants indicated the behaviors they exhibited, and these behaviors were combined to form scores on each of the four dimensions of the interpersonal circumplex (one for each pole): dominance, submissiveness, quarrelsomeness, and agreeableness. These scores provided a basis for placing behaviors in one of the quadrants of the circumplex, with quadrants defined by combinations of the dominant–submissive and quarrelsome–agreeable axes.

The quadrant in which the behavior is located represents the interpersonal style the participant exhibited during the interaction. The specific way this was defined numerically was the angular rotation of the vector representing the behavior. In simpler terms, this was the direction in which a line connecting the behavior to the origin was pointing. In addition to providing a basis for describing the interpersonal style of the participant, the scores provided a basis for knowing how strongly the participant exhibited the behaviors constituting this style. This was the length of the vector – how far from the origin (0, 0, with a behavior at the origin indicating no strength) the behavior was. So, a person could have exhibited a strong dominant–agreeable style, a weak submissive–dominant style, and so forth.

The bottom line is that Moskowitz and Zuroff were able to represent numerically what type of interpersonal style individuals exhibited during interactions and how strongly they exhibited this style.

For measures of instability, *flux* was defined as variability around an individual's mean score on a dimension, i.e., a standard deviation. A flux score was calculated for each of the four dimensions, and agency and communion, which represented combinations of the four dimensions. These measures are similar conceptually to the "traditional" measures of within-person instability I just discussed. They directly measure how inconsistent an individual was on a characteristic.

The important additional information this framework provides is a measure of how much people's interpersonal style varied across interactions. One way this variability was defined was *spin* – the within-person standard deviation of the measure of an individual's position in the circumplex, the angular rotation, which was described previously. The interpersonal style of a person with high spin moves among the quadrants more than the interpersonal style of someone with low spin. The second way that changes in interpersonal style were measured was *pulse* – the within-person standard deviation of how strongly an individual exhibited whatever style he or she was exhibiting. A person with low pulse would exhibit interpersonal styles with the same strength across interactions, whereas the strength of the interpersonal style of a person with high pulse would vary across interactions.

I will illustrate such analyses using data presented in Kuppens, Van Mechelen, Nezlek, Dossche, and Timmermans (2007). We reported the results of two studies of emotional variability. The first, a "beeper study," measured affect using the affect grid (described earlier, Russell et al., 1989). The second was an "end-of-day" study, and we measured affect using four measures: PA, NA, PD, and ND.

Listed below is the SPSS syntax for calculating flux, pulse, and spin from the data generated in the first study, which used the affect grid. Other data analysis packages have similar functions. The analyses occur in three steps. First, the raw data are recoded (if necessary) so that 0 represents the midpoint of the responses on the two dimensions. Measures of Euclidean distances are then calculated. Second, within-person summary measures are created using these measures. These measures include Pulse (the within-person SD of the strength of the affect response) and the two Flux measures (the within-person SDs of arousal and pleasantness). These data are written to a new file that can then be saved as a data set. These data can also be written to a new data set. See dialog box in SPSS. Third, using this new file, a measure of Spin is calculated.

Step 1:

/* Valence and Arousal scores need to be coded so that 0 is the midpoint for both. Initially, Valence and Arousal were represented on a 0–8 scale, so they needed to be recoded. */

/* Recode Valence and Arousal so that they range from −4 to +4 with 0 as midpoint. */

COMPUTE VAL_rcd = Valence - 4.

COMPUTE ARS_rcd = Arousal - 4.

/* Compute the Euclidean distance of each score from the midpoint, 0, 0. */

COMPUTE EucDist = SQRT((VAL_rcd * VAL_rcd) + (ARS_rcd * ARS_rcd)).

/* Transform observed vector (VAL, ARS) to unit vector by dividing each observation by the distance from the midpoint. */

COMPUTE VAL_trans=VAL_rcd/EucDist.

COMPUTE ARS_trans=ARS_rcd/EucDist.

Step 2:

/* Pulse = the within-person SD of the Euclidean distances between each point on the affect grid and the neutral midpoint, 0, 0. */

/* Within-person SDs of pleasantness and arousal are Flux. */

/* Use "Data --> Aggregate" command to get Pulse (SD of EucDist) and Sum of transformed VAL, ARS vectors. */

/* Click on box to request program to save number of observations per person, called "N_Break" by default in SPSS. Can be renamed if desired. */

/* Example – assuming data have been sorted on subjID. Created variables have been renamed – easily done in SPSS.*/

```
AGGREGATE
/OUTFILE='sum_data'
/PRESORTED
/BREAK=SubjID
/FLUX_VAL = SD(Valence)
/FLUX_ARS = SD(Arousal)
/PULSE = SD(EucDist)
/sumVal_trans = SUM(VAL_trans)
/sumARS_trans = SUM(ARSs_trans)
/N_Break=N.
```

Step 3:

/* The next two commands are executed on the AGGREGATE data set. */

/* Compute the length of R/n, where n is the person-specific number of observations. */

/* Calculate 'Spin' by taking the square root of −2 times the natural log of R. */

COMPUTE R = sqrt((sumVAL_trans * sumVAL_trans) + (sumARS_trans * sumARS_trans))/N_BREAK .

COMPUTE SPIN = sqrt(-2*ln(R)).

Mean squared successive difference

The two approaches just described have been popular ways of capturing the instability in a set of observations. I think that a way to conceptualize and measure
instability that has been developed more recently holds considerable promise.
Ebner-Priemer, Eid, Kleindienst, Stabenow, and Trull (2009) proposed a framework based upon a quantity called the mean squared successive difference
(MSSD) originally proposed by von Neumann, Kent, Bellinson, and Hart (1941).
Although their article focuses on instability within the context of psychopathology, the framework it proposes can be applied readily to the types of diaries I have
discussed in this volume.

I think that the contribution Ebner-Priemer et al. have made is potentially semi-
nal. They discuss how previous measures of instability do not take into account the
temporal (sequential) instability in a set of observations. For example, assume two
sets of 10 observations each, as shown in the table below. In terms of most measures
of stability, such as the SD, these two sets of observations would be equally unstable. For example, the mean for each set of observations is 5, and the SD is 3.16.

Data set 1		Data set 2	
Raw	$(x_{n+1} - x_n)^2$	Raw	$(x_{n+1} - x_n)^2$
2		2	
2	0	8	36
2	0	8	0
2	0	2	36
2	0	2	0
8	36	8	36
8	0	2	36
8	0	8	36
8	0	2	36
8	0	8	36

Nevertheless, looking at the two sets of observations, the first set is clearly more
stable than the second. In the first set, there is only one change, from observation
5 (2) to observation 6 (8). In contrast, in the second set of observations, there are
many more changes, from observation 1 (2) to observation 2 (8), from observation
3 (8) to observation 4 (2), and so forth. To capture such changes, Ebner-Priemer
et al. suggested using the MSDD. The formula for calculating the MSDD (δ^2) for
a set of observations (n) of variable x is given below:

$$\delta^2 = \Sigma \ (x_{n+1} - x_n)^2/(n - 1)$$

As discussed by von Neumann et al., the formula for the MSDD is the same as
the formula for the traditional measure of variance with which we are all familiar,

with one critical difference. The variance is the sum of the squared deviations from the mean divided by $n-1$, whereas the MSDD is the sum of the squares of the difference between an observation and the observation that preceded it. For the first set of data, the MSDD is 4.0. For the second set, it is 28. Note that for these examples, $n = 9$ for calculating the MSDD. There is no difference score for the first observation. Although the estimates of instability created by the MSDD may not be dramatically different than estimates based on the traditional SD, they do capture more aspects of instability than measures based on the traditional SD.

Moreover, Ebner-Priemer et al. extended the MSDD framework to the flux, pulse, and spin measures of instability proposed by Moskowitz and Zuroff. For flux, the application is relatively straightforward. Instead of calculating the "standard" SD of flux, Ebner-Priemer et al. calculated the MSDD using successive differences in flux along two dimensions. To incorporate temporality into measures of instability in terms of position within a two-dimensional circumplex, Ebner-Priemer et al. recommended using either a *Euclidean* or *Taxicab*-based algorithm. Both of these algorithms involve measuring the difference between successive observations simultaneously in two dimensions. The two methods differ in terms of how these differences are squared and combined. Ebner-Priemer et al. provide clear descriptions of the application of both methods.

By design, the MSDD incorporates the temporal sequence of a set of observations, and analysts need to be mindful of the possibility that the differences in time between successive observations may vary. At the time the article was written, von Neumann was at the Aberdeen Proving Grounds, a US weapons research facility. Von Neumann et al. were dealing with ballistics data, and so the observations with which they were concerned were gathered on a very regular basis. By the way, the reference list for this article reads like a who's who of statistics.

In contrast, as discussed by Ebner-Priemer et al., the intervals between successive observations in some types of diary studies may not be the same (or even approximately or functionally the same). For example, in a social interaction diary study, the time between successive interactions typically varies quite a lot, both between and within persons. Moreover, the events themselves occur over different amounts of time. In some ESM studies, intervals between measurement occasions may be (intentionally) random and therefore may be different.

At present, there has not been sufficient study of the MSDD to provide a firm basis for making recommendations about when and how to use it (or not use it). Nevertheless, it seems to be a valuable tool for researchers interested in the temporal dynamics of human thought, feeling, and behavior.

Time series and dynamical systems analyses

It is also possible to conceptualize within-person variation in terms of changes across time. Two sets of techniques that can do this are time series analyses and non-linear dynamical system analyses, and both seem to be positioned to become more common data analytic techniques for diary-style data. To appreciate some of the challenges facing those who apply such techniques to the analysis of the types of data typically collected by personality and social psychologists, it is useful to review briefly the genesis of these methods.

Traditionally, time series analyses have frequently been used to analyze economic and business trends, productions schedules/cycles, and various phenomena in physics, meteorology, and biology. These analyses examine long-term trends such as unemployment cycles. Using time series analyses, researchers can estimate or model trends of various types such as monthly, semi-annual, annual, or longer. You may have seen the terms "Fourier transformation" or "spectral" analysis. These are techniques that can be used to identify trends in time series data. Much of the literature on autocorrelation (see previous section on non-standard error structures) is grounded in research on time series designs.

Non-linear dynamical systems (typically referred to simply as dynamical systems these days) share with time series analyses a focus on changes across time. As suggested by the titles, however, the relationships that are examined are not linear, a phrase that includes a wide variety of possibilities. Similar to time series analyses, analyses of non-linear dynamics can require numerous observations, perhaps more than is found in your typical diary study.

Unfortunately, this is not the venue to review these techniques. If you are interested in such analyses, I recommend Deboeck (2012) as an introduction.

Some final thoughts on measures of variability/instability per se

My sense is that as more scholars become more aware of different ways of conceptualizing and measuring instability as an individual difference, research on this topic will expand. As attractive as a construct may be, unless researchers know how to set up studies and analyze the data they collect, they are unlikely to pursue a certain topic. Nevertheless, I respectfully suggest that individuals who study instability per se take into account the following conceptual and statistical issues.

Conceptually, I think researchers need to consider the possibility that the relationship between instability and adjustment is not simply linear. That is, an individual who does not vary at all – who feels the same and thinks the same about him- or herself across time and situations – could be described as rigid and unresponsive to the environment. When people fail, they should feel worse than when they succeed, and as suggested by research on the sociometer model (e.g., Leary, Tambor, Terdal, & Downs, 1995), when they are rejected they should feel less well about themselves. People should vary. As is often the case, it would seem that questions about instability need to concern what is too little and what is too much?

There is also the issue of the consistency of instability across domains (different constructs). As noted previously, Gable and Nezlek (1998) suggested that the instability of self-esteem (which had been considered on its own) might be a manifestation of a more general construct of instability. Based on daily measures, individual differences in the instability of self-esteem were positively correlated with the instability of anxiety, perceived control over the environment, depressogenic adjustment, and causal uncertainty. These relationships were such that these various measures of instability constituted an instability factor.

Moreover, I have done a series of analyses (presently unpublished) on other data sets in which essentially the same result occurred. In factor analyses, measures of instability (within-person SDs) of various measures (affect, self-focused, and FFM) taken at the day level loaded on the same factor even when means of these measures loaded on different, multiple factors. It should be noted that the within-person relationships between these measures were "all over the map." Some were high, some were low. When considered as a scale, these measures of instability also constituted a reliable scale ($\alpha = .92$). Although such results are preliminary, they support the belief that instability is some type of general tendency. Individuals who vary on one construct seem to vary on others, irrespective of the relationships between the constructs themselves. See Eid and Diener (1999) for a similar analysis of within-person variability in affect only.

Perhaps more important is the issue of the construct that measures of within-person variability per se represent. Responses over time may vary for a few reasons. First, there is unreliability. Unless a measure is perfectly reliable (1.0), even if the underlying construct being measured does not change, the observed measures will vary. Second, and quite important for the types of diary data I have discussed in this volume, there is the influence of external circumstances. For a study such as a daily diary study, this could mean what happened each day. For a social interaction diary study, this could mean the other people who were present. Third, there may be individual differences in how people react to events and circumstances. When faced with the same stress, two individuals may react differently.

Although one can assume that measurement error is randomly distributed across persons and occasions, it seems unlikely that external circumstances and reactivity to events do not vary systematically across persons. Therefore, measures of instability per se represent a combination of random and non-random factors. Admittedly, at some level of analysis, one might simply be satisfied with knowing that some people are more unstable than others, but it would seem to be of interest to understand such differences in a bit more detail.

8

In conclusion and some thoughts about the future

There can be little doubt that diary methods have become and are likely to remain an important part of the set of research methods used by social and personality psychologists as well as a wide variety of other researchers. Diary methods provide numerous and important advantages over both single assessment (one-shot) surveys and lab methods, and simply due to the nature of the techniques these advantages are not going to disappear. They are inherent in the techniques and in the nature of the data provided by these techniques.

As recording technologies become more sophisticated and less expensive, I suspect that the data collected in diary studies will evolve to include more objective measures that do not rely upon self-report. Moreover, I suspect that these new technologies will include measures of the environment (à la the EAR). I do not think self-reports will be eliminated; rather, these new data will complement self-reports. It is difficult to imagine a psychological science that does not place some value on the phenomenology of the individual.

Technological advances are also changing how people interact, how they relate to each other, and so forth, and I think researchers need to acknowledge the fact that people are spending more and more time in the "cyber world," for lack of a better term. The use of chat rooms, blogs, social networking, texting, instant messaging, and so forth, is on the rise, and not just in developed countries, but across the world at large. Importantly, the dynamics underlying such computermediated communication are likely to be different from the dynamics underlying face-to-face contact. Given all this, it would seem to be wise to incorporate (in some way) cyber reality into diary studies. By the way, if you read the literature on cyber communication you will see the abbreviations FTF and CMC for face-to-face and computer-mediated-communication respectively.

Incorporating the cyber world will be challenging for a number of reasons. First, such technologies are developing and changing rapidly. What is popular today may be unheard of a year from now. This means that data collection protocols will need to be flexible enough to incorporate such changes, but sufficiently stable to provide a basis for drawing conclusions that go beyond the specific technologies being studied. Second, cyber events (including interactions) may be very brief and occur very often during a day, and the ratio of information to noise (in terms of extracting psychological meaning) may be low. Someone may send and receive dozens of SMS messages each day, and we will have to develop ways of understanding and measuring the psychological importance of these communication episodes.

Our models and the research examining them have largely relied upon face-to-face contact. For example, in the studies I have done using the Rochester Interaction Record, interactions have been explicitly limited to face-to-face contact. The rationale has been that the dynamics of face-to-face contact are different from the dynamics of computer-mediated-communication, and, historically, computer-mediated-communication was not that prominent a part of people's lives. Admittedly, some types of social contact were lost, but this loss was deemed to be unimportant.

I offer the following as an example of studying the cyber world. Recently, a graduate student of mine conducted a daily diary study on computer-mediated-communication (Kovaz, 2011). Each day, participants described the social contacts they had that were computer-mediated-communications. These descriptions included the mode (IM, SMS, etc.), the person with whom the participants were communicating, and so forth. Also, they provided additional ratings of what they considered to be the most important episode. Preliminary analyses suggested that life in the cyber world (at least as represented by computer-mediated-communication) paralleled life in the actual world. Relationships between traits such as social anxiety and reactions to computer-mediated-communication were similar to the results found between social anxiety and reactions to face-to-face contact. Regardless of this specific result, as a discipline, we need to find ways of incorporating cyber life into real life. Although it will be challenging, I think it is possible and will prove to be quite valuable.

In terms of data analysis, I think that the type of multilevel modeling analyses I have described here will remain a standard for a good time to come. The statistical theory underlying the modeling techniques is well established, the algorithms are stable, and so forth. Moreover, the framework is sufficiently flexible to accommodate various procedures, and such procedures are being developed and published continually. I suspect that one of the more important developments in the multilevel framework will be a more complete integration of multilevel modeling and structural equation modeling. Although multilevel structural equation modeling (MSEM) exists now, there is still much work to be done, but it is simply a matter of time before this occurs.

Although multilevel modeling is likely to remain a standard approach, I suspect that analyses relying upon non-linear dynamics will become more widely used. This will require better instruction about non-linear dynamics, more theoretical models that incorporate non-linear dynamics, more studies that are designed to test such models, and more accessible software to do the analyses. Nevertheless, as more researchers know more about non-linear dynamics, it is difficult to imagine that psychology will not follow other sciences in which the use of non-linear dynamics has increased markedly over the past few decades.

Well, that does it for now. Please accept my best wishes for success in your work.

Appendix 1
Sample social interaction diary instructions

This appendix contains a sample set of instructions that I have used in a social interaction diary study. Typically, participants are given a set of instructions similar to these at an introductory meeting, and how to complete the forms is explained. The groups are small enough (20 or less) to reduce the psychological distance between researchers and participants. If the data are collected electronically (e.g., a website), how to use the website should be illustrated. If not, an explanation of the pencil and paper forms should be given. At all times, researchers should emphasize the collaborative nature of the research.

Instructions for the Daily Interaction Form

During the next two weeks, please describe all your social interactions that last 10 minutes or more. Whether you are on campus or not, whatever you are doing, describe your social interactions using the record. The more consistent and reliable your recording is, the more valid our inferences about the data become. It is most important that you keep the record *every day, all the time*. Participants in other studies like this one have found it useful to update the record sometime in the afternoon and in the evening before they retire. Regardless, you need to update the record every day, at least once a day. The entire study depends on your cooperation in keeping these records. Even if you feel that a certain day was completely routine with nothing out of the ordinary, record it. If you have lunch with the same people every day, record it every day.

For this study, a social interaction is defined as any situation involving you and one or more other people in which the behavior of each person is affected by the behavior of the others. A conversation is probably the best example of an interaction, although interactions do not have to include constant conversation; for example, going for a walk with someone is an interaction. Just being with other people and not interacting with them is not an interaction. For example, sitting with someone and watching television and not talking with that person would not be an interaction. The most important consideration is this: If you and the other people influence each other, if you change your behavior *in response* to their behaviors, or if they change their behavior in response to you, then an interaction has occurred. Participants in past research have not had much difficulty in determining what an interaction was and we think you will find it pretty easy also.

Please describe your interactions using the form [on the website]. The form is easy to complete, but we have included the following instructions in case any questions arise. For all your interactions, answer all the questions on the form. Your answers will provide a very good description of your general patterns of behavior.

Describe *ALL* interactions using the online form.

Date: *ALWAYS* record the day and month when the interaction occurred. You need to include this information every time you fill out the form, NOT just on the first form of that day.

Time: Enter the time the interaction started (00:00–24:00).

Length: Record how long the interaction lasted in hours and/or minutes.

Nature

For this response, click on the one that best describes what was going on. The choices are:

- Simple Conversation
- Meal

Reg. Meal – this is a planned meal with one or more persons that occurs at the same time every day/every Tue. and Thurs./every week. For example, if you eat lunch with your roommate every Monday at 12pm at the café, you would choose this category.

Socializing – this is an activity where meeting and talking to other people is the primary goal. For example, going to the pub on a Friday night is socializing.

Relaxation – this is an activity where you are not intending to socialize necessarily. For example, playing a game of tennis is an interaction but your primary goal is not to talk per se.

- Date
- Party
- Work
- Meeting
- Studying

Exchanging PA – this is an exchange of physical affection (such as kissing, making out, sexual intercourse, etc.).

Other – for example, church, bus ride, etc.

Location

For this topic, click on the primary location where the interaction took place. If the interaction took place in two locations, list the one that was most important or where the majority of the interaction took place. For example, if you meet someone at a pub but then you walk back to your room and proceed to talk for an hour, you would click on My room. The choices are:

- My room
- My dormitory
- Other dormitory
- UC or Campus Center
- Other on-campus
- Off-campus, local
- Off-campus, not local
- Other

People you were with

Initials – Record the initials of the other people in the interaction. If two people have the same initials, distinguish them with a middle initial (if you know it) or by the second letter of their last name. As an example, if you list Jack Kramer as J.K. then James Kennedy would be J.K.E. The most important thing is to be consistent. Once you describe James Kennedy as J.K.E., always do that, otherwise we will not know who certain initials represent. If you do not know a certain person's name or only one initial, you may assign them a set of initials that you will remember. For example, if you met a girl at work but did not catch her name, you could call her W.G. (for work girl). Even if you interacted with her again and found out her name, you would still use W.G. to refer to her. If you are having problems, come up with a master code list of all your interactants to refer to when making your daily entries. Also, click on whether they are male or female.

Relationship – Record the relationships that are most salient. For example, if you work with a close friend, then you would describe this person as a close friend, not as other because he or she was a co-worker. Your choices are:

- Roommate – this also includes housemates and suitemates.
- Casual Friend – this is someone you see regularly but that you are not overly close to. This could be your lab partner or a club member.
- Close Friend

- Romantic Partner – this is someone that you see/date on a regular basis or is someone that you are intimate with regardless of commitment.
- Stranger
- Other – this can include a professor, your TA, etc.

Group – If there were more than three other people present you should not record their initials on the form. Instead, you should indicate the number (excluding yourself) of females and males.

Your reactions to and perceptions of interactions

For each interaction, describe your reactions to it and record your perceptions of it. Scales are provided on the form.

Enjoyable: This is an indication of how much you enjoyed the interaction and how satisfying you felt it to be. Putting a "1" would indicate that the interaction was not at all enjoyable or satisfying, whereas a "9" would indicate that the interaction was very enjoyable and satisfying.

Exchange Opinions: This is an indication of how free you felt to exchange/offer opinions, ideas, and attitudes during the interaction and the extent to which you did so. A score of "1" would indicate that you did not exchange any ideas/opinions nor did you feel okay doing so, whereas a "9" would indicate that you freely exchanged ideas and felt comfortable doing so.

Respected/valued: This is an indication of the degree to which you felt respected and valued as a person in the opinion of the person(s) with which you were interacting. A score of "1" would mean that you did not feel respected or valued at all while a score of "9" would signify that you felt very respected and valued by that person(s).

Intimacy: This scale indicates how close you felt to the other people present and how intimate you felt the interaction was. Such closeness or intimacy does not have to be sexual, nor does it have to be evident only through conversation. Sometimes actions speak louder than words and you may feel that you are close to someone more because of how they behave than because of what they say. If you felt an interaction was very intimate, record a "9," whereas if you felt it was not at all intimate, record a "1."

Liked: This is an indication of the degree to which you felt the people you were interacting with liked you. People may vary in how much they like you at different times (this is true even of your close friends) so it is important to notice how much everyone you interact with seems to like you during all your interactions. If you felt they really liked you, you would record a "9," but if you felt that they did not like you at all during the interaction you would record "1."

Influential: This is an indication of how influential you felt during the interaction. This may vary as a function of the setting in which you are in and the people you are around. Meetings where your ideas are accepted and praised often make you feel influential. In contrast, sometimes, it seems more appropriate to just sit back and listen (like listening to your roommate drone on and on about her problems while not taking any of your advice). If you felt very influential, you would record a "9" whereas if you did not feel influential at all, you would record a "1."

Like an Outsider: This measure is designed to determine the extent to which you felt outside of the interaction. Often, despite being engaged in a conversation, you really do not feel like you are a part of what is going on. This can be especially true in group interactions. This is not necessarily negative – perhaps you are not really interested in what is going on. Unlike the above measures, the scoring on this measure is opposite. A score of "1" means that you did not feel like an outsider at all whereas a score of "9" would mean that you very much so felt like an outsider.

Long interactions

There may be occasions when you are with one person or in a group for an extended period of time. If you feel that there was really just one interaction, record it as such. However, often, a long interaction should be divided into shorter interactions.

For example, you and a close friend spend 3–4 hours together. Over this time, you may have a meal, watch TV, go to a movie, and study. To the extent that is possible, divide this long period of time into separate interactions, each describing a different part of the time you and your friend spent together. Common ways to divide this long time might be changes in location or activity; however, you should divide the time using distinctions that are meaningful to you.

Even relatively short periods of social contact may be ambiguous. You meet a friend A.B. and have a 15-minute conversation. You notice that it is lunchtime and have lunch together, which lasts for 30 minutes. If the quality of your interaction with A.B. did not change very much when you went to lunch, you should record one event of 45 minutes. If you feel that things changed, you should record two interactions, one of 15 minutes, another of 30 minutes, both of which occurred with A.B. How would you describe the event – as a casual conversation or eating lunch together? This would depend on how you thought of the event. You could recall the meeting as "A.B. and I ate lunch together after we met talking across campus" or "A.B. and I really had quite a conversation which continued into lunch," and both interpretations would be accurate.

Sometimes, people will enter and leave an ongoing interaction. You are with a friend, J.O., for one hour, just walking and talking around campus. Another friend, P.D., joins you and J.O. for 20 minutes and then leaves. You and J.O. are together for an hour and then go your separate ways. This sequence of events should be recorded as three separate interactions: one with J.O. for 60 minutes, a second with

J.O. and P.D. for 20 minutes, and a third with J.O. for 60 minutes. You would fill out three sets of ratings, one for each event. If you and J.O. had not met P.D., you probably would have recorded the event as one interaction of 140 minutes in length.

If you have any questions or need anything clarified, please feel free to contact me either by email or by phone. And again, thank you for your participation. [Contact information]

If You Miss A Day: If you miss a day (completely), please continue the study the next day by logging on as usual with that day's interactions, not those of the day before. DO NOT make up the missed interaction forms by doing it the next day. The computer notes the time and duration of all your responses.

Confidentiality: The data and results from this study will be kept strictly confidential. Only XXX will have access to your answers. Your name will never be associated with any of your responses or with the results of the study. The Internet site is secure, and your responses are not accessible to anyone but the researchers.

A Few Other Notes: Please realize that it may take longer the first few times you log on and fill out the forms. Once you are used to the process, however, it will be a very short process of 5–10 minutes (depending on how many interactions you have). Your thoughtful participation each day will be greatly appreciated.

Appendix 2

Diary-level measures

In this appendix, I present various measures that have been used in diary-style studies in which I have been involved. Note that these studies have all used an end-of-day report. This list is not meant to be exhaustive in the slightest. It is meant to be illustrative of what can be done. Unless noted otherwise, scale scores are the means for the responses constituting that scale, with reversals when appropriate. Researchers will need to modify stems (the introductory phrase for a set of items) and response scales as appropriate.

Daily events

In the daily diary studies I have done I have always put a measure of daily events at the beginning of the end-of-day reports. My sense is that describing what happened each day provides a good context for remembering other aspects of the day itself, such as how people felt and so forth. Such a sequence may also minimize the influence of something that just happened a few minutes ago or very recently.

The schedule of events below is a modification of a schedule originally presented by Butler, Hokanson, and Flynn (1994). They had 40 items, some of which were eliminated.

As discussed in the main body of the text, the event schedule was designed to produce four separate scores: positive social events (e.g., items 1 and 7), negative social events (e.g., items 4 and 16), positive achievement (e.g., items 2 and 10), and negative achievement (e.g., items 12 and 20). See main text for a discussion of scoring events.

Sample instructions and items for a daily study with end-of-day report

A series of events that commonly occur in the lives of students will follow. Please read each carefully. Some of the events may have occurred in your life today, some may not have occurred today.

If the event did NOT occur today, enter 0.

If the event did occur today, rate how important it was to you using the following scale:

1 = Not important
2 = Somewhat important
3 = Pretty important
4 = Extremely important

_____	1	Had especially good interactions with friend(s) or acquaintances.
_____	2	Completed work on an interesting project or assignment.
_____	3	Did poorly on schoolwork task (e.g., test, assignment, job duty).
_____	4	Did something awkward or embarrassing in a social situation.
_____	5	Was excluded or left out by my group of friends.
_____	6	Fell behind in coursework or duties.
_____	7	Went out socializing with friends/date (e.g., party, dance club).
_____	8	Met a daily fitness goal.
_____	9	Had especially good interactions with my steady date.
_____	10	Performed well (sports, music, speaking, drama, etc.).
_____	11	A disagreement with a close friend or steady date was left unresolved.
_____	12	Classmate, teacher, co-worker, or friend criticized me on my abilities.
_____	13	Did something special for a friend/steady date that was appreciated.
_____	14	Flirted with someone or arranged a date.
_____	15	Got caught up (or ahead) in coursework or work duties.
_____	16	Got along poorly with peers (e.g., classmates, co-workers, roommates).
_____	17	Failed to meet a daily fitness goal.
_____	18	Classmate, teacher, co-worker, or friend complimented me on my abilities.
_____	19	Went out to eat with a friend/date.
_____	20	Tried to do homework and could not understand it.
_____	21	Did well on a school or work task (e.g., test, assignment, job duty).
_____	22	Had plans fall through to spend time with someone special.
_____	23	Had other type of pleasant event (not listed above) with friends, family, or date.
_____	24	Had other type of unpleasant event (not listed above) with friends, family, or date.
_____	25	Had other type of pleasant event (not listed above) concerning performance at school, work, or another activity.
_____	26	Had other type of unpleasant event (not listed above) concerning schoolwork, or another activity.

Self-esteem

The daily measure below is based on Rosenberg's (1965) classic 10-item trait scale. Out of deference to tradition, the daily scale below uses the agree–disagree response option. Typically, there are seven response options. The first two items are reversed. See Nezlek and Gable (2001) for some psychometrics.

Listed below are a number of statements concerning personal attitudes and characteristics. Please read each statement and consider the extent to which you agree or disagree thinking about yourself today. All responses will be kept confidential, so please answer as honestly as possible. Remember, base your responses on the extent to which you agree or disagree with each statement as it describes how you felt today.

Today…

1 All in all, I was inclined to feel like a failure. REVERSE
2 I took a positive attitude toward myself. REVERSE
3 On the whole, I was satisfied with myself.
4 At times I thought I was no good at all.

Depressogenic adjustment

In numerous studies I have administered a daily measure of what I have come to call "depressogenic adjustment" based on Beck's "Triad" – feelings about self, life in general, and the future (e.g., Beck, 1972). Note the different response scales to accommodate the differences in the items. See Nezlek and Gable (2001) for some psychometrics.

1 Overall, how positively did you think about yourself today?

    1 = very negatively
    2 = negatively
    3 = somewhat negatively
    4 = neither negatively nor positively
    5 = somewhat positively
    6 = positively
    7 = very positively

2 Thinking of your life in general, how well did things go today?

    1 = very poorly
    2 = poorly
    3 = somewhat poorly
    4 = neither poorly nor well
    5 = somewhat well
    6 = well
    7 = very well

3 How optimistic are you about how your life (in general) will be tomorrow?

   1 = very pessimistic
   2 = pessimistic
   3 = somewhat pessimistic
   4 = neither pessimistic nor optimistic
   5 = somewhat optimistic
   6 = optimistic
   7 = very optimistic

Self-consciousness/Self-focused attention

Given Trapnell and Campbell's (1999) research distinguishing positive self-focused attention (reflection) from negative self-focused attention (rumination) at the trait level, I recommend distinguishing these at the state level also. The public self-conscio usness items presented below were based on the trait items presented in Feningstein, Scheier, and Buss's (1975) original article, and the rumination and reflection items were based on the trait items presented in Trapnell and Campbell (1999). A brief discussion of these scales is in Nezlek (2005).

For each of the statements below indicate how much time you spent thinking about each of the following topics or things today. Use the scale below.

   1 = very little, 2 = some amount, 3 = quite a lot of time, 4 = almost all the time

Public self-conscious:

1 Thinking about your physical appearance (clothes, grooming, etc.).
2 Thinking about what other people thought of you.?
3 Thinking about making a good impression on other people.?

Rumination:

1 How much time did you spend "ruminating" or dwelling on things that happened to you for a long time afterward?
2 Today I played back over in my mind how I acted in a past situation.
3 How much time did you spend rethinking things that are over and done with?

Reflection:

1 How much today did you think about the nature and meaning of things?
2 How much did you care today for introspective or self-reflective thinking?
3 Today, how much did you think about your attitudes and feelings?

Self-concept clarity

In Nezlek and Plesko (2001) we measured daily self-concept clarity based on the trait scale offered by Campbell et al. (1996).

For each of the statements below, indicate how well they characterized you today.

- My beliefs about myself often conflict with one another.
- Sometimes I feel that I am not really the person I appear to be.
- My beliefs about myself seem to change frequently.

Empathy

In Nezlek, Feist, Wilson, and Plesko (2001), we measured daily empathy using the four items below, based on Mehrabian (1996).

- The sadness of a close one rubbed off on me.
- I did not overly become involved with friends' problems.
- I was not affected easily by the strong emotions of people around me.
- Another's happiness was uplifting for me.

Need for cognition

In Nezlek et al. (2001), we measured need of cognition using the items below, based on Cacioppo and Petty (1982).

- I would prefer simple to complex problems.
- I like to have the responsibility of handling a situation that requires a lot of thinking.
- Thinking is not my idea of fun.
- I would rather do something that requires little thought than something that is sure to challenge my thinking abilities.

Mood and affect

Diary-level measures of mood (and in combination, affect) will vary widely as a function of researchers' specific interests. I have listed below the items I have used in much of my research. These items are intended to provide measures of the affective circumplex as discussed by Feldman Barrett and Russell (1998). Items from the four subscales are presented in mixed order. You can calculate a mean response for each of the four scales or combine them to get a positive vs. negative score and an active vs. deactive score. See Nezlek et al. (2008b) for an analysis of the psychometrics of the 16 items presented below, including cultural comparisons.

Using seven-point scales with endpoints labeled "Did not feel this way at all" and "Felt this way very strongly," and a midpoint (4) labeled "Felt this way moderately," participants describe how they felt that day.

- Positive active affect: enthusiastic, happy, proud, alert, and excited.
- Positive deactive affect: calm, satisfied, relaxed, peaceful, and content.
- Negative active affect: nervous, stressed, tense, upset, and embarrassed.
- Negative deactive affect: depressed, sluggish, sad, bored, and disappointed.

Causal uncertainty

As presented by Weary and Edwards (1994), causal uncertainty refers to people's perceived ability to predict or explain causal relationships in their worlds. In parallel with the conceptualization of daily events as positive–negative + social–achievement, the daily measure presented below asks respondents to describe how uncertain they were in terms of four life domains. Nevertheless, the four items constitute a reliable diary-level measure (.72, see Nezlek & Gable, 2001). The questions below are intended for a response magnitude estimation scale (e.g., 1 = not all, 7 = very much, with labeled midpoints).

Thinking back on your day today in terms of the positive interactions you had with others, how well did you did understand why things happened as they did?
    Repeat above question and change target:

- positive non-social events (e.g., schoolwork, sports, etc.) that occurred.
- negative interactions I had with others.
- negative non-social events (e.g., schoolwork, sports, etc.) that occurred.

Psychological needs and authenticity

In Heppner et al. (2008) we measured daily needs based upon the work of Sheldon, Elliot, Kim, and Kasser (2001), and daily authenticity based on Kernis and Goldman (2006). In this study, we used an agree–disagree response scale.

- Today I felt...
- (Autonomy)
- That my choices were based on my own interests and values
- That my choices expressed my "true self"
- (Competence)
- That I was taking on and mastering hard challenges

- Very capable in what I did
- (Relatedness)
- Close and connected with other people who are important to me
- A strong sense of intimacy with the people I spent time with
- (Authenticity)
- That I wore a number of social "masks" (reverse scored)
- That throughout the day I was in touch with my "true self"

Causality orientation

Based on Deci and Ryan's (1985) concept of causality orientation, the following items were administered. See Nezlek and Gable (2001) for a discussion of the analyses of these items.

For each of the following questions please indicate the degree to which you felt about each statement today.

SCALE: 1 = No extent   2 = Small extent   3 = Moderate extent   4 = Great extent

1 Thinking back on your day today in terms of social events that occurred and the relationships you have with others, to what extent did you feel that you had a choice about what you did and to what extent did things happen the way you wanted them to happen?
2 Thinking back on your day today in terms of non-social areas of performance (e.g., schoolwork, sports, fitness, etc.), to what extent did you feel that you had a choice about what you did and to what extent did things happen the way you wanted them to happen?
3 Thinking back on your day in terms of social events that occurred and the relationships you have with others, to what extent were you able to control the outcomes of these events?
4 Thinking back on your day in terms of non-social areas of performance (e.g., schoolwork, sports, fitness, etc.), to what extent were you able to control the outcomes of these events?

References

Affleck, G., Zautra, A., Tennen, H., & Armeli, S. (1999). Multilevel daily process designs for consulting and clinical psychology: A preface for the perplexed. *Journal of Consulting and Clinical Psychology, 67,* 746–754.

Aiken, L. S., & West, S. G. (1991). *Multiple regression: Testing and interpreting interactions.* Newbury Park, CA: Sage.

Barnett, R. C., Marshall, N. L., Raudenbush, S. W., & Brennan, R. T. (1993). Gender and the relationship between job experiences and psychological distress: A study of dual-earner couples. *Journal of Personality and Social Psychology, 64,* 794–806.

Baron, R. A., & Kenny, D. M. (1986). The moderator-mediator variable distinction in social psychological research: Conceptual, strategic, and statistical considerations. *Journal of Personality and Social Psychology, 51,* 1173–1182.

Barta, W. D., Tennen, H., & Litt, M. (2012). Measurement reactivity in diary research. To appear in M. R. Mehl & T. S. Conner (Eds.), *Handbook of research methods for studying daily life* (pp. 108–123). New York: Guilford Press.

Bauer, D. J., Preacher, K. J., & Gil, K. M. (2006). Conceptualizing and testing random indirect effects and moderated mediation in multilevel models: New procedures and recommendations. *Psychological Methods, 11,* 142–163.

Baumeister, R. F., Bratslavsky, E., Finkenauer, C., & Vohs, K. D. (2001). Bad is stronger than good. *Review of General Psychology, 5,* 323–370.

Beck, A. T. (1972). *Depression: Causes and treatment.* Philadelphia: University of Pennsylvania Press.

Blascovich, J. J., Vanman, E., Mendes, W. B., & Dickerson, S. (2011). Social psychophysiology for social and personality psychology. In J. B. Nezlek (Ed.), *The SAGE library in social and personality psychology methods.* London: Sage.

Bolger, N., Davis, A., & Rafaeli, E. (2003). Diary methods: Capturing life as it is lived. *Annual Review of Psychology, 54,* 579–616.

Bolger, N., Stadler, G., & Laurenceau, J. P. (2012). Power analysis for diary and intensive longitudinal studies. In M. R. Mehl & T. S. Conner (Eds.), *Handbook of research methods for studying daily life* (pp. 285–301). New York: Guilford Press.

Bryk, A. S., & Raudenbush, S. W. (1992). *Hierarchical linear models.* Newbury Park, CA: Sage.

Butler, A. C., Hokanson, J. E., & Flynn, H. A. (1994). A comparison of self-esteem lability and low trait self-esteem as vulnerability factors for depression. *Journal of Personality and Social Psychology, 66,* 166–177.

Cacioppo, J. T., & Petty, R. E. (1982). The need for cognition. *Journal of Personality and Social Psychology, 42,* 116–131.

Campbell, J. D., Trapnell, P. D., Heine, S. J., Katz, I. M., Lavallee, L. F., & Lehman, D. R. (1996). Self-concept clarity: Measurement, personality correlates, and cultural boundaries. *Journal of Personality and Social Psychology*, *70*, 141–156.

Carter, B. L., Day, S. X., Cinciripini, P. M., & Wetter, D. W. (2007). Momentary health interventions: Where are we and where are we going? In A. A. Stone, S. Shiffman, A. A. Atienza, & L. Nebeling (Eds.), *The science of real-time data capture: Self-reports in health research* (pp. 289–307). New York: Oxford University Press.

Cliff, N. (1959). Adverbs as multipliers, *Psychological Review*, *66*, 27–44.

Cranford, J. A., Shrout, P. E., Iiada, M., Rafaeli, R., Yip, T., & Bolger, N. (2006). A procedure for evaluating sensitivity to within-person change: Can mood measures in diary studies detect change reliably? *Personality and Social Psychology Bulletin*, *32*, 917–929.

Csikszentmihalyi, M., & Larson, R. (1987). Validity and reliability of the experience-sampling method. *Journal of Nervous and Mental Disease*, *175*, 526–536.

Deboeck, P. R. (2012). Modeling non-linear dynamics in intraindividual variability. In M. R. Mehl & T. S. Conner (Eds.), *Handbook of research methods for studying daily life* (pp. 440–458). New York: Guilford Press.

Deci, E. L., & Ryan, R. M. (1985). The General Causality Orientations Scale: Self-determination in personality. *Journal of Research in Personality*, *19*, 109–134.

Delespaul, P. (1995). *Assessing schizophrenia in daily life: The experience sampling method*. Maastricht: Maastricht University Press.

DePaulo, B. M., Kashy, D. A., Kirekndol, S. E., Wyer, M. M., & Epstein, J. A. (1996). Lying in everyday life. *Journal of Personality and Social Psychology*, *70*, 979–995.

Ebner-Priemer, U. W., Eid, M., Kleindienst, N., Stabenow, S., & Trull, T. J. (2009). Analytic strategies for understanding affective (in)stability and other dynamic processes in psychopathology. *Journal of Abnormal Psychology*, *118*, 195–202.

Eid, M., & Diener, E. (1999). Intraindividual variability in affect: Reliability, validity, and personality correlates. *Journal of Personality and Social Psychology*, *76*, 662–676.

Enders, C. K., & Tofighi, D. (2007). Centering predictor variables in cross-sectional multilevel models: A new look at an old issue. *Psychological Methods*, *12*, 121–138.

Feldman Barrett, L., & Russell, J. A. (1998). Independence and bipolarity in the structure of current affect. *Journal of Personality and Social Psychology*, *74*, 967–984.

Feningstein, A., Scheier, M. F., & Buss, A. (1975). Public and private self-consciousness. *Journal of Consulting and Clinical Psychology*, *43*, 522–527.

Fleeson, W. (2001). Toward a structure- and process-integrated view of personality: Traits as density distributions of states. *Journal of Personality and Social Psychology*, *80*, 1011–1027.

Gable, S. L., & Nezlek, J. B. (1998). Level and instability of day-to-day psychological well-being and risk for depression. *Journal of Personality and Social Psychology*, *74*, 129–138.

Gable, S. L., & Reis, H. T. (1999). Now and then, them and us, this and that: Studying relationships across time, partner, context, and person. *Personal Relationships*, *6*, 415–432.

Gable, S. L., & Reis, H. T. (2010). Good news! Capitalizing on positive events in an interpersonal context. In M. Zanna (Ed.), *Advances in experimental social psychology, 42* (pp. 198–257). New York: Elsevier.

Goffman, E. (1971). *Relations in public*. New York: Basic Books.

147

Heatherton, T. F., & Polivy, J., (1991). Development and validation of a scale for measuring state self-esteem. *Journal of Personality and Social Psychology, 60,* 895–910. doi: 10.1037/0022-3514.60.6.895

Heppner, W. L., Kernis, M. H., Nezlek, J. B., Foster, J., Lakey, C. E., & Goldman, B. M. (2008). Within-person relationships between daily self-esteem, need satisfaction, and authenticity. *Psychological Science, 19,* 1140–1145. doi: 10.1111/j.1467-9280.2008.02204.x

Hufford, M. R. (2007). Special methodological challenges and opportunities in ecological momentary assessment. In A. A. Stone, S. Shiffman, A. A. Atienza, & L. Nebeling (Eds.), *The science of real-time data capture: Self-reports in health research* (pp. 54–75). New York: Oxford University Press.

Kanner, A. D., Coyne, J. C., Schaefer, C., & Lazarus, R. S. (1981). Comparison of two modes of stress measurement: Daily hassles and uplifts versus major life events. *Journal of Behavioural Medicine, 4,* 1–39.

Kenny, D. A., Kashy, D. A., & Cook, W. L. (2006). *Dyadic data analysis.* New York: Guilford Press.

Kernis, M. H. (2005). Measuring self-esteem in context: The importance of stability of self-esteem in psychological functioning. *Journal of Personality, 73,* 1569–1606.

Kernis, M. H., & Goldman, B. M. (2006). A multicomponent conceptualization of authenticity: Theory and research. In M. P. Zanna (Ed.), *Advances in experimental social psychology* (Vol. 38): New York: Elsevier.

Kovaz, D. (2011). *Social compensation, social enhancement, and rejection in everyday online conversations.* Unpublished masters thesis, College of William & Mary, Williamsburg, VA.

Kreft, I. G. G., & de Leeuw, J. (1998). *Introducing multilevel modeling.* Newbury Park, CA: Sage.

Kuppens, P., Van Mechelen, I., Nezlek, J. B., Dossche, D., & Timmermans, T. (2007). Individual differences in core affect variability and their relationship to personality and psychological adjustment. *Emotion, 7,* 262–274.

Leary, M. R., Nezlek, J. B., Downs, D., Radford-Davenport, J., Martin, J., & McMullen, A. (1994). Self-presentation in everyday interactions: Effects of target familiarity and gender composition. *Journal of Personality and Social Psychology, 67,* 664–673.

Leary, M. R., Tambor, E. S., Terdal, S. K., & Downs, D. (1995). Self-esteem as an interpersonal monitor: The Sociometer Hypothesis. *Journal of Personality and Social Psychology, 68,* 513–530.

Littell, R. C., Milliken, G. A., Stroup, W. W., & Wolfinger, R. D. (1996). *SAS system for mixed models.* Cary, NC: SAS Institute.

Mehl, M. R. (2007). Eavesdropping on health: A naturalistic observation approach for social health research. *Social and Personality Psychology Compass, 1*(1), 359–380. doi: 10.1111/j.1751-9004.2007.00034.x

Mehl, M. R., & Conner, T. S. (Eds.). (2012). *Handbook of research methods for studying daily life.* New York: Guilford Press.

Mehl, M. R., Pennebaker, J. W., Crow, M., Dabbs, J., & Price, J. (2001). The Electronically Activated Recorder (EAR): A device for sampling naturalistic daily activities and conversations. *Behavior Research Methods, Instruments, and Computers, 33,* 517–523.

Mehrabian, A. (1996). *Manual for the Balanced Emotional Empathy Scale (BEES).* [Available from Albert Mehrabian, 1130 Alta Mesa Road, Monterey, CA 93940, USA.]

Mohr, C. D., Armeli, S., Tennen, H., Carney, M. A., Affleck, G., & Hromi, A. (2001). Daily interpersonal experiences, context, and alcohol consumption: Crying in your beer and toasting good times. *Journal of Personality and Social Psychology, 80,* 489–500.

Moskowitz, D. S. (1994). Cross-situational generality and the interpersonal circumplex. *Journal of Personality and Social Psychology, 66,* 921–933.

Moskowitz, D. S., & Zuroff, D. C. (2004). Flux, pulse, and spin: Dynamic additions to the personality lexicon. *Journal of Personality and Social Psychology, 86,* 880–893.

Nezlek, J. B. (1993). The stability of social interaction. *Journal of Personality and Social Psychology, 65,* 930–942.

Nezlek, J. B. (2000). The motivational and cognitive dynamics of day-to-day social life. In J. P. Forgas, K. Williams, & L. Wheeler (Eds.), *The social mind: Cognitive and motivational aspects of interpersonal behaviour* (pp. 92–111). New York: Cambridge University Press.

Nezlek, J. B. (2001). Multilevel random coefficient analyses of event and interval contingent data in social and personality psychology research. *Personality and Social Psychology Bulletin, 27,* 771–785.

Nezlek, J. B. (2002). Day-to-day relationships between self-awareness, daily events, and anxiety. *Journal of Personality, 70,* 249–275.

Nezlek, J. B. (2003). Using multilevel random coefficient modeling to analyze social interaction diary data. *Journal of Social and Personal Relationships, 20,* 437–469.

Nezlek, J. B. (2005). Distinguishing affective and non-affective reactions to daily events. *Journal of Personality, 73,* 1539–1568.

Nezlek, J. B. (2007a). Multilevel modeling in research on personality. In R. Robins, R. C. Fraley, & R. Krueger (Eds.), *Handbook of research methods in personality psychology* (pp. 502–523). New York: Guilford Press.

Nezlek, J. B. (2007b). A multilevel framework for understanding relationships among traits, states, situations, and behaviors. *European Journal of Personality, 21,* 789–810.

Nezlek, J. B. (2011). Multilevel modeling for social and personality psychology. In J. B. Nezlek (Ed.), *The SAGE library in social and personality psychology methods.* London: Sage.

Nezlek, J. B., & Allen, M. R. (2006). Social support as a moderator of day-to-day relationships between daily negative events and daily psychological well-being. *European Journal of Personality, 20,* 53–68.

Nezlek, J. B., Feist, G. J., Wilson, F. C., & Plesko, R. M. (2001). Day-to-day variability in empathy as a function of daily events and mood. *Journal of Research in Personality, 35,* 401–423.

Nezlek, J. B., & Gable, S. L. (2001). Depression as a moderator of relationships between positive daily events and day-to-day psychological adjustment. *Personality and Social Psychology Bulletin, 27,* 1692–1704.

Nezlek, J. B., Hampton, C. A., & Shean, G. D. (2000). Clinical depression and everyday social interaction in a community sample. *Journal of Abnormal Psychology, 109,* 11–19.

Nezlek, J. B., Imbrie, M., & Shean, G. D. (1994). Depression and everyday social interaction. *Journal of Personality and Social Psychology, 67,* 1101–1111.

Nezlek, J. B., Kafetsios, K., & Smith, C. V. (2008a). Emotions in everyday social encounters: Correspondence between culture and self-construal. *Journal of Cross-Cultural Psychology, 39,* 366–372. doi: 10.1177/0022022108318114

Nezlek, J. B., & Pilkington, C. J. (1994). Perceptions of risk in intimacy and everyday social interaction. *Personal Relationships, 1,* 45–62.

Nezlek, J. B., & Plesko, R. M. (2001). Day-to-day relationships among self-concept clarity, self-esteem, daily events, and mood. *Personality and Social Psychology Bulletin, 27,* 201–211.

Nezlek, J. B., & Plesko, R. M. (2003). Affect- and self-based models of relationships between daily events and daily well-being. *Personality and Social Psychology Bulletin, 29,* 584–596.

Nezlek, J. B., & Schaafsma, J. (2010). Understanding the complexity of everyday interethnic contact: Recommendations for researchers. *Social and Personality Psychology Compass, 4*(10), 795–806. doi: 10.1111/j.1751-9004.2010.00302.x

Nezlek, J. B., Schaafsma, J., Safron, M., & Krejtz, I. (in press). Self-construal and the inter- and intraethnic social interactions of ethnic minorities. *Journal of Cross-Cultural Psychology,* doi:10.1177/0022022111399647

Nezlek, J. B., Schütz, A., & Sellin, I. (2007). Self-presentational success in daily social interaction. *Self and Identity, 6,* 361–379.

Nezlek, J. B., Sorrentino, R. M., Yasunaga, S., Otsubo, Y., Allen, M., Kouhara, S., & Shuper, P. (2008b). Cross-cultural differences in reactions to daily events as indicators of cross-cultural differences in self-construction and affect. *Journal of Cross-Cultural Psychology, 39,* 685–702. doi: 10.1177/0022022108323785

Nezlek, J., & Wheeler, L. (1984). RIRAP: Rochester Interaction Record Analysis Package. *Psychological Documents,* 14, p. 6, fiche 2610.

Nezlek, J. B., Wesselman, E., Williams, K. D., & Wheeler, L. (in press). Ostracism in everyday life. *Group Dynamics.*

O'Grady, M. A., Cullum, J., Armeli, S., & Tennen, H. (2011). Putting the relationship between social anxiety and alcohol use into context: A daily diary investigation of drinking in response to embarrassing events. *Journal of Social and Clinical Psychology, 30,* 599–615.

Osgood, C. E., Suci, G. J., & Tannenbaum, P. H. (1957). *The measurement of meaning.* Urbana, IL: University of Illinois Press.

Pennebaker, J. W., Booth, R. J., & Francis, M. E. (2007). *Linguistic inquiry and word count: LIWC 2007.* Austin, TX: LIWC (www.liwc.net).

Preacher, K. J., Zyphur, M. J., & Zhang, Z. (2010). A general multilevel SEM framework for assessing multilevel mediation. *Psychological Methods, 15,* 209–233.

Radloff, L. S. (1977). The CES-D scale: A self report depression scale for research in the general population. *Applied Psychological Measurement, 1,* 385–401.

Raudenbush, S. W., & Bryk, A. S. (2002). *Hierarchical linear models* (2nd ed.). Newbury Park, CA: Sage.

Reis, H. T. (2012). Why researchers should think "real-world": A methodological and conceptual rationale. In M. R. Mehl & T. S. Conner (Eds.), *Handbook of research methods for studying daily life* (pp. 3–21). New York: Guilford Press.

Reis, H. T., & Gable, S. L. (2000). Event-sampling and other methods for studying everyday experience. In H. T. Reis & C. M. Judd (Eds.), *Handbook of research methods in social and personality psychology* (pp. 190–222). New York: Cambridge University Press.

Richter, T. (2006). What is wrong with ANOVA and multiple regression? Analyzing sentence reading times with hierarchical linear models. *Discourse Analysis, 41,* 221–250.

Robins, R. W., Hendin, H. M., & Trzesniewski, K. H. (2001). Measuring global self-esteem: Construct validation of a single-item measure and the Rosenberg self-esteem Scale. *Personality and Social Psychology Bulletin, 27*, 151–161.

Rosenberg, M. (1965). *Society and the adolescent self-image.* Princeton, NJ: Princeton University Press.

Russell, J. A., Weiss, A., & Mendelsohn, G. A. (1989). Affect grid: A single-item scale of pleasure and arousal. *Journal of Personality and Social Psychology, 57*, 493–502.

Sarason, I. G., Johnson, J. H., & Siegel, J. M. (1978). Assessing the impact of life changes: Development of the Life Experiences Survey. *Journal of Consulting and Clinical Psychology, 46*, 932–946.

Schaafsma, J., Nezlek, J. B., Krejtz, I., & Safron, M. (2010). Ethnocultural identification and naturally occurring interethnic social interactions: Muslim minorities in Europe. *European Journal of Social Psychology, 40*, 1010–1028. doi: 10.1002/ejsp.699

Schwartz, J. E., & Stone, A. A. (2007). The analysis of real-time momentary assessment data: A practical guide. In A. A. Stone, S. Shiffman, A. A. Atienza, & L. Nebeling (Eds.), *The science of real-time data capture: Self-reports in health research* (pp. 54–75). New York: Oxford University Press.

Sheldon, K. M., Elliot, A. J., Kim, Y., & Kasser, T. (2001). What is satisfying about satisfying events? Testing 10 candidate psychological needs. *Journal of Personality and Social Psychology, 80*, 325–339.

Singer, J. D. (1998). Using SAS PROC MIXED to fit multilevel models, hierarchical models, and individual growth models. *Journal of Educational and Behavioral Statistics, 23*, 323–355.

Smith, C. V., Nezlek, J. B., Webster, G. D., & Paddock, E. L. (2007). Relationships between daily sexual interactions and domain-specific and general models of personality traits. *Journal of Social and Personal Relationships, 24*, 497–515.

Snijders, T., & Bosker, R. (1999). *Multilevel analysis.* London: Sage.

Spielberger, C. D., Gorsuch, R. L., & Lushene, R. E. (1970). *Manual for the state-trait anxiety inventory.* Palo Alto, CA: Consulting Psychologists Press.

Stone, A. A., Shiffman, S., Atienza, A. A., & Nebeling, L. (2007a). Historical roots and rationale of Ecological Momentary Assessment (EMA). In A. A. Stone, S. Shiffman, A. A. Atienza, & L. Nebeling (Eds.), *The science of real-time data capture: Self-reports in health research* (pp. 54–75). New York: Oxford University Press.

Stone, A. A., Shiffman, S., Atienza, A. A., & Nebeling, L. (Eds.). (2007b). *The science of real-time data capture: Self-reports in health research* (pp. 54–75). New York: Oxford University Press.

Stone, A. A., Turkkan, J. S., Bachrach, C. A., Jobe, J. B., Kurtzman, H. S., & Cain, V. S. (Eds.). (2000). *The science of self-report: Implications for research and practice.* Mahwah, NJ: Lawrence Erlbaum.

Trapnell, P. D., & Campbell, J. D. (1999). Private self-consciousness and the five factor model of personality: Distinguishing rumination from reflection. *Journal of Personality and Social Psychology, 76*, 284–304.

Verduyn, P., Delvaux, E., Van Coillie, H., Tuerlinckx, F., & Van Mechelen, I. (2009). Predicting the duration of emotional experience: Two experience sampling studies. *Emotion, 9*, 83–91.

von Neumann, J., Kent, R. H., Bellinson, H. R., & Hart, B. I. (1941). The mean square successive difference. *Annals of Mathematical Statistics, 12*, 153–162.

Weary, G., & Edwards, J. A. (1994). Individual differences in causal uncertainty. *Journal of Personality and Social Psychology, 67*, 308–318.

West, S. G., Ryu, E., Kwok, O. M., & Cham, H. (2011). Multilevel modeling: Current and future applications in personality research. *Journal of Personality, 79*, 1–50.

Wheeler, L., & Miyake, K. (1992). Social comparison in everyday life. *Journal of Personality and Social Psychology, 62*, 760–773.

Wheeler, L., & Nezlek, J. (1977). Sex differences in social participation. *Journal of Personality and Social Psychology, 35*, 742–754.

Wheeler, L., & Reis, H. (1991). Self-recording of everyday life events: Origins, types, and uses. *Journal of Personality, 59*, 339–354.

Wiggins, J. S. (1991). Agency and communion as conceptual coordinates for the under-standing and measurement of interpersonal behavior. In W. M. Grove & D. Cicchetti (Eds.), *Thinking clearly about psychology* (pp. 89–113). Minneapolis: University of Minnesota Press.

Index